947
Modern

MODERN WORLD NATIONS

Russia

Second Edition

William A. Dando
with additional text by Zoran Pavlović

Series Editor
Charles F. Gritzner
South Dakota State University

An imprint of Infobase Publishing

Frontispiece: Flag of Russia

Cover: View of the Cathedral of Christ the Savior, with the Moskva River in the foreground, Moscow.

Russia, Second Edition

Copyright ©2007 by Infobase Publishing

All rights reserved. No part of this book may be reproduced or utilized in any form or by any means, electronic or mechanical, including photocopying, recording, or by any information storage or retrieval systems, without permission in writing from the publisher. For information contact:

Chelsea House
An imprint of Infobase Publishing
132 West 31st Street
New York NY 10001

ISBN-10: 0-7910-9248-8
ISBN-13: 978-0-7910-9248-4

Library of Congress Cataloging-in-Publication Data
Dando, William A., 1934-
  Russia / William A. Dando with additional text by Zoran Pavlovic. — 2nd ed.
     p. cm. — (Modern world nations)
  Includes bibliographical references and index.
  ISBN 0-7910-9248-8 (hardcovers)
  1. Russia (Federation)—Juvenile literature. I. Title. II. Series.
  DK510.23.D36 2007
  947—dc22   2006035395

Chelsea House books are available at special discounts when purchased in bulk quantities for businesses, associations, institutions, or sales promotions. Please call our Special Sales Department in New York at (212) 967-8800 or (800) 322-8755.

You can find Chelsea House on the World Wide Web at http://www.chelseahouse.com

Series and Cover design by Takeshi Takahashi

Printed in the United States of America

Bang Hermitage 10 9 8 7 6 5 4 3 2 1

This book is printed on acid-free paper.

All links, Web addresses, and Internet search terms were checked and verified to be correct at the time of publication. Because of the dynamic nature of the Web, some addresses and links may have changed since publication and may no longer be valid.

Table of Contents

Russia

Second Edition

1

Introducing Russia

I cannot forecast to you the action of Russia.
It is a riddle wrapped in a mystery inside an enigma.
—Winston Churchill

Throughout the past century, Russia and the United States have been at the center of world political and economic events. In 1904–05, Russia fought Japan in the Russo-Japanese War. The president of the United States, Theodore Roosevelt, helped bring about peace between the two nations in 1905. From 1914 to 1918, Russia took part in World War I, which weakened the nation and led to food shortages that helped cause the Russian Revolution in 1917. This revolution eventually led to the birth of the Soviet Union—a Communist country—in 1922. Then Germany invaded the Soviet Union in June 1941 during World War II. Winning the war in 1945, and subsequent development of nuclear technology, made the Soviet Union, along with its former ally the United States, superpowers. For many years, the two superpowers competed to have more influence and better technology than the other. This contest was called the cold war. Russians launched Sputnik, the first satellite, in 1957. They sent the first human, Yuri Gagarin, into space, in 1961. These uses of Soviet technology impressed the whole world.

In April 1986, a tragic accident at the Chernobyl Nuclear Power Plant in Ukraine shattered the myth of Soviet scientific strength. After this event, many of the 15 republics that made up the Soviet Union began to question whether they wanted to remain in the union. This, combined with political weaknesses and a stagnant economy in the late 1980s, brought about major changes. By the early 1990s, these factors led to the breakup of the Communist bloc (nations under Soviet influence) and the emergence of free, democratic countries in central Europe. These events caused the disintegration of the Soviet Union. In December 1991, Russia became an independent, democratic nation. It was the largest and most powerful member of a new loose confederation of the nations from the former Soviet Union, which was called the Commonwealth of Independent States (CIS). After the fall of the Soviet Union, Russia was no longer a superpower. Even so, Russia is still a powerful nation today, and it continues to play an important role in world affairs and the global economy.

Geographic location has played an important role in Russian history and culture. It has both helped and hindered the expansion and economic growth of this vast territory. Russia is located in both Europe and Asia. Its western quarter lies in Europe. Its eastern three-quarters lie in Asia. Asian Russia—past and present—has been rather remote in geographic terms. Its borders are formed by often ice-locked seas and towering mountain ranges.

Russia is the world's largest country. The Soviet Union was even larger. Size alone, however, does not equal strength. It can actually create problems. Russia is challenged to organize and

Russia is a vast country that covers one-eighth of the earth's surface and stretches across 11 time zones. It is the world's largest country; nearly twice the size of the second-largest nation, Canada.

control such an immense area. It must maintain transportation and communication links. It must make distant and vastly different areas part of a functioning whole.

Russia covers an area of 6.6 million square miles (17 million square kilometers). It is 82 percent larger than the United States. From east to west, the country spans 170 degrees of longitude and 11 time zones. This is the only country on which the sun is always shining somewhere. Russia stretches 5,600 miles (9,000 kilometers) from the Polish border on the Baltic Sea in the west to the Bering Strait in the Pacific Ocean in the east. The distance from Severnaya Zemlya, an island in the Arctic Ocean, to the nation's southernmost point near the 45th parallel is about 3,100 miles (5,000 kilometers).

With 143 million people, Russia has the world's sixth-largest population. However, there are only 21 Russians per square mile (8 per square kilometer), roughly one-third the population density of the United States.

After the revolution, the Soviet Union attempted to remold the sprawling Imperial Russian Empire. The Communist Party sought to change the nation's geographic conditions, including its economy, settlement, and linkages. Communist leaders used Marxist centralized national planning to make changes. To pull together the scattered, ethnically diverse population, they built new systems. Roads, railroads, canals, and air routes were constructed. Thousands of new cities brought people together. State and cooperative farms changed rural life. More land was cultivated.

However, many people still lacked basic services. Necessary goods were hard to get. The people came to realize that existing political and economic systems could not cope with the complex issues of modern economic life. Massive discontent ultimately broke the control of the Communist Party. Like earlier rulers, Communist Party leaders failed to overcome the problems posed by Russia's vast space and diversity. They failed to

In December 1991, the Soviet Union was officially dissolved and split into 15 independent republics, including Russia. Here, Russian schoolchildren sit atop a statue of former Communist leader Joseph Stalin in a Moscow park, shortly before the Communist government was overthrown.

bring the many diverse cultures of the huge Soviet Union together as one nation. In December 1991, the Soviet Union collapsed under the weight of its inefficiencies.

The legacy of the Soviet past has not yet been totally erased. In the years since the demise of the Soviet Union, Russia has made many social, economic, and political changes. Democracy, capitalism, privatization, and market reform underlie the new post-Soviet economic scene. Today, Russia is emerging as a partner of the United States. The two countries now recognize how important they can be to one another. Western politicians, Western business interests, and the United Nations are paying a great deal of attention to Russia, a fascinating country that is taking its rightful place on today's global stage.

2

Physical Landscapes

WEATHER AND CLIMATE

The landscape of Russia is impacted greatly by its climate. In particular, temperature extremes characterize Russia's weather. Low winter temperatures have a tremendous impact on basic physical processes and human activities. Extremes in temperature and low annual precipitation are a direct result of Russia's high latitudinal position and of its location in the northern part of Asia, the world's largest landmass.

Russia's weather and climate are so severe that scientists have devoted much time to studying them. One Russian geographer-scientist was Vladimir Köppen. He is considered the "father of modern climatology," the study of climates. Born in Russia in 1846, Köppen became deeply interested in the climate of the steppes. The steppes are vast grasslands that extend almost all the way across the country. In St. Petersburg, where he did his research, he created the first world

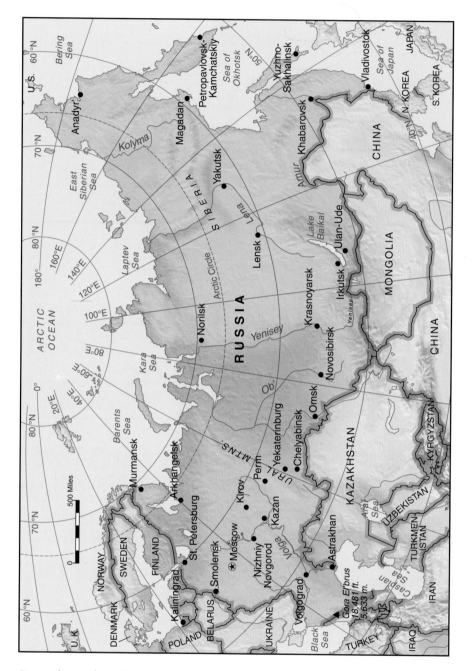

Due to its northern latitude, Russia is the coldest country on Earth. The majority of Russia is composed of vast plains, with the exception of the southern part of the country, which is quite mountainous along the borders with Kazakhstan and Turkey.

map of temperature belts in 1884. Scientists throughout the world were soon using this map. In 1900, Köppen created a system to classify climates. Köppen was also a biogeographer. He studied the influence of weather and climate upon the distribution of plants. His background led him to create a classification that was, in part, a descriptive vegetation region system. He used the letters A, B, C, D, and E to identify his climates.

Köppen's Major Climatic Regions

A   tropical rainy climates (forests); not found in Russia

B   dry climates

BW for wasteland or deserts

BS for grasslands or steppe

C   midlatitude rainy climates with mild winters (deciduous forests)

D   midlatitude rainy climates with cold winters (evergreen forests)

ET polar tundra climates (moss, lichens, or ice)

Köppen wrote that weather changes from day to day, but that climate changes very slowly. Climate, according to Köppen, describes and integrates the averages, totals, and extremes of weather over long periods of time. The two most important climatic factors are temperature and precipitation.

ET Climates: Subpolar or Tundra

The ET or tundra climate is found along Russia's Arctic coast, from the Norwegian border to the Bering Strait that separates Russia from Alaska. During at least one month of the year, this climatic region experiences an average temperature above 32°F (0°C). No month has an average temperature higher than 50°F

(10°C). Weather is severe, and strong winds continually sweep across a landscape that has little vegetation. Winters are long, and there is no sunlight for several months. Precipitation ranges from 6 to 12 inches annually (15 to 31 centimeters). Widespread swamps form where permanently frozen ground prevents subsurface drainage.

D Climates, or Humid Continental

D climates with short summers and long, severe winters characterize most of Russia. These climates occupy a zone 1,000 to 1,200 miles (1,609 to 1,931 kilometers) wide south of the ET climate belt, from the Polish border to the Pacific Ocean. The coldest month averages 32°F (0°C) or below. The warmest months exceed 50°F (10°C). Winters are very long and very cold. Temperatures below freezing prevail for at least five to six months in most places—particularly in Siberia. Precipitation is limited. It ranges from an annual average of 32 inches (81 centimeters) along the western border to 12 inches (31 centimeters) in central Siberia. This climate in Siberia coincides with the Russian "taiga," the largest continuous area of forest on Earth.

C Climates, or Subtropical

C climates are the mildest found in Russia. Only a few areas, such as the northern Caucasus region, the southernmost point in Russia, enjoy this pleasant climate. The coldest month averages less than 65°F, but remains well above freezing. Temperatures for the warmest months exceed 72°F (22°C). Amounts of precipitation vary from 22 inches to 32 inches (56 to 81 centimeters) a year, and in seasonal distribution. Less than one percent of the total area of Russia has this climate type.

BS Climates, or Dry Steppe

The BS or dry steppe climates are found in a belt south of the forests of southern Russia. Broad, flat, dry, grassy plains characterize this region. Precipitation is limited. It averages between 10 and 20 inches (25 to 51 centimeters) a year. Normally, the amount of precipitation is less than the potential evaporation. Because evaporation is excessive, there is little water to help plants develop. Droughts are frequent. Average annual temperatures vary greatly.

BW Climates, or Very Dry Desert

The BW, or very dry desert climate, characterizes areas north of the Caspian Sea. Rainfall averages of 8 inches (20 centimeters) or less mean precipitation is more meager and more erratic than in the BS (steppe) climate. As in the BS climate, there are "hot" and "cold" deserts, depending on temperature. Humidity is low and skies usually are clear of clouds. Dryness here is not only related to annual rainfall totals, but also to a function of evaporation that is closely dependent upon temperature. As temperatures increase, so does evaporation. Cloudless skies, nearly 85 percent of the year, and low humidity allow maximum sunlight and heating during the day. At night, however, heat rapidly radiates (escapes) back into space. Thus, day and night temperatures range greatly.

Other Complex Climatic Regions

Russia also has other complex climatic regions. They include the "undifferentiated highland climates" found in mountainous regions. Here, altitudinal zonation (elevation differences) creates climatic bands that extend from the base of mountains to their tops. Different climates also are found on northern and southern slopes.

A distinct "monsoon" climate is found along the coastal regions of the Far East, from Vladivostok northward to the Amur River. Average annual precipitation ranges from about 25 to 40 inches (64 to 102 centimeters). Most of it falls during the summer. Temperatures in this monsoon climate are mild for the latitude. Also, most major cities have distinct "urban climates," which are warmer and drier than surrounding areas. At times, there are unusual winter "urban fogs." The burning of fossil fuels creates water droplets that condense into ground clouds.

NATURAL VEGETATION

Vladimir Köppen believed that the natural vegetation native to an area reflects the total physical environment of that place. There are nine vegetation regions in the huge Russian cultural realm. Seven are major east-west vegetal belts. Two are formed by a unique combination of special physical conditions. The total forest area is estimated at 2.9 million square miles (4.7 million square kilometers). These vegetal belts progress from north to south in the order listed below.

Tundra

The tundra is a belt of distinctive plants and shrubs that forms a continuous strip from the Norwegian border to the Kamchatka Peninsula. Almost everywhere, permafrost (permanently frozen subsoil) lies beneath it. Climatic conditions are too severe for most trees to survive. Tundra vegetation typically consists of mosses, lichens, sedges, hearty grasses, and dwarf bushes. In a few sites, stunted birch trees do grow. Flooded areas and shallow basins in this region are most often swamps. On the southern edge of this belt, the size and number of plants increase as growing conditions improve.

Taiga

Across a wide band of Russia—more than 4,000 miles (6,437 kilometers) from the Gulf of Finland in the west to the Sea of Okhotsk in the east, and at least 800 miles (1,288 kilometers) wide—is a magnificent, unbroken forest composed of spruce, fir, larch, and pine. This vegetal belt, called the taiga, is bounded on the north by the southern fringe of the tundra. The mixed and deciduous forests of European Russia and the wooded steppe of western Siberia border the taiga on the south. The most valuable portion of the taiga is in Europe. Here, Norway spruce, Scotch pine, and Siberian fir are the dominant trees. Birch is a common deciduous tree found on both the northern and southern fringes of the taiga. Permafrost conditions in Siberia limit the type of trees that can grow. The Siberian larch, a deciduous needleleaf, is the dominant tree there.

Mixed and Deciduous Forests

South of the taiga, in the western portion of the Russian cultural realm, is a wedge of mixed and deciduous forests. The base of this triangular wedge follows the western borders of Estonia, Latvia, Lithuania, Belarus, and Ukraine, and its tip is at the crest of the Ural Mountains in Russia. Conifers dominate in the northern sector of this wedge. Broadleaf deciduous trees are dominant in the southern sector. Pine, spruce, fir, ash, elm, linden, birch, oak, beech, and maple are found in the northern European portion of the mixed and deciduous forest. Tall trees are rare. Another kind of forest is found on the slopes of the Caucasus Mountains. Oak, ash, poplar, pine, and spruce, as well as broadleaf evergreens are found here. In the Far East of Russia, the forest has conifers and hardwoods, along with Japanese and Manchurian species. A hearty northern bamboo is also found in the Far East. The western wedge has been heavily timbered, and much of its forest cleared for agriculture.

Wooded Steppe

Between the mixed and deciduous forests and the taiga of the north, and the semidesert and desert vegetal bands of the south, lies a vast expanse of wooded steppe and steppe grasslands. The wooded steppe is a transition vegetal zone that extends across a narrow band of southern Russia and northern Ukraine into western Siberia. It is composed of small, isolated

Birch tree forests dot the wooded steppe of southern Siberia. These small to medium-size trees generally live in northern temperate climates and are closely related to the beech and oak family. Pictured here is a stand of birch and pine trees along the Yenisey River between the towns of Krasnojarsk and Jenisseisk.

forests or clumps of oak, birch, and aspen separated by patches of tall grassland. Other than drought-tolerant pine, needleleaf coniferous trees generally are not found in the wooded steppe. The western or Ukrainian-Russian wooded steppe is characterized by broadleaf deciduous trees. Birch trees characterize the Siberian wooded steppe. Humans have impacted most of the wooded steppe in some way. The beautiful tall grasses have been, for the most part, plowed under. The land is now planted with winter wheat or sunflowers.

Steppe

South of the wooded steppe is the true steppe, a continuous belt of short grasses that extends from western Russia to southwest

Siberia and Kazakhstan. Trees here are confined to river valleys or where planted and maintained. This vegetal belt has warmer, longer summers than the wooded steppe. The frost-free period is longer, but there is less precipitation. Recurrent droughts and fires caused by lightning or humans kill most trees. Short grasses and bunch grasses are the only vegetation that can survive and flourish. Where it is plowed and improperly managed, the soil suffers from wind erosion.

Semidesert

The steppe grassland blends southward into the semidesert. Short grasses, low bunch grasses, and widely spaced bushes slowly replace bunch grasses. As the climate becomes drier and the summer temperatures increase, grasses eventually disappear, and trees are found only in river valleys. Evaporation of the soil's limited moisture draws salt to the surface. A shallow, soft layer of white salt covers swales and other lowland areas. Only salt-tolerant plants can survive these natural evaporation pans.

Desert

South of the semidesert is the true desert, where vegetation is scant and species limited. As the climate becomes hotter and drier in summer, year-round grasses disappear. Widely spaced, drought-resistant bushes become dominant. The desert vegetal region gives parts of south-central Russia a characteristic landscape. Winters are cold. Very strong winds mark periods of seasonal change. Dust storms are common. Where there is soil, desert shrubs that are physiologically equipped to withstand drought through special roots, stems, and leaves grow far apart. Other desert plants depend entirely upon small, erratic amounts of rainfall. They germinate after one rainstorm, produce a beautiful carpet of flowers, and after a short life duration, they die. Desert vegetation has little value for grazing animals.

Subtropical Forests

In stark contrast to the grasslands and deserts of the Volga Delta region are the beautiful subtropical forests of the western Caucasus Black Sea coast. Luxuriant tall evergreens, stately deciduous trees, thick vines, tall firs, and even palm trees and a form of bamboo abound. The climate in the foothills of the Caucasus Mountains near the Black Sea is warm, humid, and very conducive to plant growth.

Mountain Grasslands

Scattered throughout Russia are areas of lush, mountainous grasslands. They appear at heights of 3,000 to 4,500 feet (914 to 1,372 meters). From 4,500 feet to 6,000 feet (1,372 to 1,829 meters), these mountain grasslands change with elevation. First, they give way to subalpine vegetation. Then, belts of moss and lichens appear. Finally, only bare outcrops of rock occur. Temperature, moisture, bedrock, relief, and wind determine altitudinal vegetation zones on mountains.

SOILS OF RUSSIA

Agriculture and food production were very important to Russian tsars. Russian scientists were encouraged to study soils and classify them according to food productivity. The "father of soil science" was Vasily Dokuchaev. He was born in Russia in 1846. In 1883, he wrote a book called *Russian Chernozem*. Dokuchaev believed that chernozem (which means "black earth") soils were created by the mutual activity of air, water, and plants. He revolutionized soil science by focusing upon the interrelated roles of climate and vegetation in soil development. Dokuchaev's soil classification system has been widely accepted around the world.

Chernozem

Chernozem soils, like Chestnut soils, have a fine, granular texture and similar basic color tones. However, they differ markedly in terms of organic matter and fertility. Chernozem was formed in an east-west belt of Russia that receives more annual rainfall than the Chestnut soil belt of the dry steppe region. It also has more moderate temperatures. Chernozem soils are formed under tall grass cover, whereas Chestnut soils form under short grass cover. Vast amounts of organic material of grass root origin extend for great depths into the upper layer of the soil. Within this mixture of mineral earth and natural compost, there is a layer of lime. Enriched by vast amounts of humus and lime, the basic parent material and wind-deposited fine silt combine to produce one of the most fertile soils in the world. The soil gets its black color from its high humus content. In this soil belt east of the Volga River and in Kazakhstan, the true Chernozem soil is not as deep, but the humus content increases to more than 15 percent. When properly managed, the soil can produce winter and spring wheat, rye, barley, oats, sugar beets, and a great variety of other crops. Chernozem soil is wonderfully fertile, and is by far the best soil for farming in Russia.

LANDFORMS AND PHYSIOGRAPHIC REGIONS

Because of its vast size, Russia contains rocks and minerals from almost every geologic period. Lev Berg, born in Russia in 1876, was an outstanding physical geographer. He was the most respected physiographic scientist in both imperial Russia and the Soviet Union. Berg believed that Russia's physiographic regions had formed over millions of years. They resulted from involved processes that took place on very complex geologic structures. Russia has 11 basic physiographic regions. Each of these has a distinctive physical character, as well as distinctive opportunities (or limitations) for human habitation. Russia's various configurations—its plains, hills and mountains, rivers, lakes, and inland seas—are important factors. They must be considered in any plan for regional or national economic development.

Russian Plain

Western Russia, located west of the Urals and south of the European Arctic Lowlands, is within the vast Russian Plain. This huge plain is basically flat and glacially modified, with poor internal drainage. Most of the plain is lower than 650 feet (198 meters) above sea level. The low, rolling, glacially created Valdai Hills are the source of the Volga and many other rivers. Near the center of this region are the Smolensk-Moscow Hills. They encompass the large but minerally poor Moscow Basin. Noted for its valuable salt deposits, the Caspian Depression lies at 92 feet (28 meters) below sea level. The shore of the Caspian Sea is the lowest place in Russia. As a result of continental glaciation, the Russian Plain lacks mineral energy resources in the north. In the south, however, it contains significant deposits of coal, minerals, and natural gas.

European Arctic Lowlands

To the north of the Russian Plain are the flat and swampy European Arctic Lowlands. Located in northwestern Russia, these lowlands are snow- and ice-covered in the winter, and retain snowmelt water on the surface in the summer. Only a few feet of soil thaw out during the summer. The underlying, permanently frozen ground (called permafrost) will not absorb meltwater. On the large Kola Peninsula adjoining Finland, repeated glacial action has carved picturesque fjords. The landscape contains thousands of small lakes, swamps, and streams. To the east and near the Ural Mountains lies the Pechora Plain. Here, coal is mined in permanently frozen ground.

North Caucasus Mountains

South of the Russian Plain, the North Caucasus Mountains and valley region are a complex mixture of spectacular landform types. The Caucasus Mountains stretch from the Black Sea to the Caspian Sea—800 miles (1,288 kilometers). Numerous mountain peaks exceed 12,000 feet (3,658 meters). Mount

Elbrus, Russia's highest peak, reaches an elevation of 18,481 feet (5,633 meters). More than 20 alpine glaciers descend from the towering, snow-clad peak. The Caucasus Mountains are a barrier to human interaction. There is only one major highway through a 700-mile (1,127-kilometer) stretch of the mountains. This mountain range is considered the southeastern limit of Europe.

Ural Mountains

East of the Russian Plain lie the historic Ural Mountains. Located within Russia, the Urals are a long, narrow, heavily eroded, low chain of mountains and hills. Their crest forms the boundary between Europe and Asia. The Urals extend more than 1,500 miles (2,414 kilometers) from north of the Arctic Circle to the deserts north and east of the Caspian Sea. They are only about 50 miles (81 kilometers) wide in the north. In the south, they spread out nearly 140 miles (225 kilometers). Consisting of a series of north-south ridges with many low east-west mountain passes, the Urals do not block human movement. Geologically, the mountains are old, have a complex structure, and abound in mineral resources. For centuries, the Urals have been extremely important to the Russian economy. This mountain range provides timber, oil, natural gas, iron ore, and a host of valuable minerals and precious metals.

West Siberian Lowland

East of the Ural Mountains is a vast area of low-lying swamps and broad floodplains called the West Siberian Lowland. This region is one of the most impenetrable, least-developed, flattest, and most monotonous portions of Earth's surface. It extends east of the Urals for more than 1,000 miles (1,609 kilometers). It spans more than 1,200 miles (1,931 kilometers) from south of the Siberian Arctic Lowland to the Caspian Basin. This vast, marshy lowland is so flat that elevation within the entire region varies no more than 400 feet (122 meters).

The broad, sluggish, meandering, northward-flowing Ob River and its tributaries drain the area. Winters are cold and harsh in the northern section of the plain. Spring thaws affect the frozen southern portions of the north-flowing rivers first. Spring and summer snowmelt water spills onto the vast flat lowland, causing widespread flooding. The southern edge of this region is covered by vast, flat steppes that are the best farming areas in all of Siberia. The unique geology of the lowland has given it some of the most productive oil and gas fields in the world.

North Caspian Basin (Desert Region)

South of the West Siberian Lowland is the dry Caspian Basin. This desert or semidesert region has internal drainage. It was once a part of Turkistan, and later, Soviet Central Asia. The dry lowland basin is formed of almost-horizontal deposits of sand, wind-deposited loess, and clay. Humans who live in the Caspian Basin experience an unusual climatic regime. They are subject to "Egyptian summers and Siberian winters."

Southwestern Asiatic Ranges

The Southwestern Asiatic ranges form a long, narrow region that begins with the Altai Mountains. These mountains extend northwestward into southwestern Siberia. Beautiful alpine glaciers and vast snowfields are characteristic of the area. The Altai Mountains average 6,000 to 6,500 feet (1,829 to 1,981 meters) in elevation. Snowmelt feeds the headwater tributaries of the mighty Ob River. North of the Altai Mountains are the Sayan Mountains. Their elevations vary from 8,500 feet (2,591 meters) in the west to 10,500 feet (3,200 meters) in the east. They form a southward-facing arc of mountains formed from granite and schist. Wedged between the Altai and Sayan ranges is the mineral-rich Kuznetsk Basin. Immense deposits of coal and iron ore have been found here. The Minusinsk Basin, located in the north-central Sayans, is a rich agricultural region that abounds in lignite, coal, and iron ore.

Siberian Arctic Lowland

East of the northern Ural Mountains is a series of flat lowlands that are snow-covered in winter and swampy in summer. Due to permafrost and poor drainage, snowmelt water and ice-dammed river water lie on the soil's surface during the summer. Open tundra vegetation, marshes, and swamps cover the Siberian Arctic Lowland. Insects abound in summer. Many of the sediments deposited by marine action bear oil and natural gas. The Ob, Yenisey, Khatanga, Lena, Yana, Indigirka, and Kolyma rivers flow northward across this flat plain. They bring sediment and summer flooding. Precious metals, including gold and silver, have been found in this sediment.

Central Siberian Plateau

North of the Central Asiatic ranges, east of the West Siberian Plain, and south of the Siberian Arctic Lowland is the Central Siberian Plateau. The Yenisey River marks the western boundary of this region. The Lena River is its approximate eastern boundary. The plateau is stream-dissected and glacially molded of limestone and clay. This upland region has elevations in excess of 1,600 feet (488 meters) above sea level. Numerous rivers have cut deep gorges into the Central Siberian Plateau. These provide great sites for hydroelectric power plant development. The plateau's complex geology and the lack of deep glacial scouring have left valuable mineral deposits near the surface. Limestone and dolomite bedrock with volcanic pipes yield large quantities of diamonds. Vast deposits of mineral fuels, iron ore, nickel, and copper lie beneath other areas.

Lena Basin

Between the Central Siberian Plateau and Eastern Highlands is the Lena Basin. This is a very complex region with rich deposits of coal, oil, natural gas, and precious metals. This basin is drained by one of the major rivers in Siberia—the Lena. The Lena River has its source on the slopes of the Baikal Mountains, near the Mongolian border. It flows northeast 2,653 miles (4,270 kilometers) to the Laptev Sea. In the summer months, it is navigable for about 2,000 miles (3,219 kilometers). Weather in the winter is severe. The Lena Basin is the driest and coldest of any Russian physiographic region. Gold has been obtained from this basin for more than a century.

Eastern Highlands

East of the Lena Basin and along the Siberian Pacific coast are the vast Eastern Highlands. Extending from Lake Baikal to the Bering Strait, this region includes the deepest lake on Earth, a complex system of mountains composed primarily of very old metamorphic and volcanic rock, and many broad intervening basins. The Kamchatka Peninsula is a unique subregion in itself. Beautiful, high mountains and snow-covered active volcanoes dot the peninsula. Geologists are currently studying 28 active volcanoes there. Numerous hot springs make this region very similar to the Yellowstone Basin in the western United States. Huge rift valleys were created by strong earthquake activity in the past. Lake Baikal, the oldest and deepest lake in the world, occupies one of these rift valleys. More than one mile deep, it is 395 miles (636 kilometers) long and 50 miles (81 kilometers) wide. It contains one-fifth of the world's surface freshwater. East of Lake Baikal, igneous and metamorphic rocks form the cores of various mountain ranges. Volcanic cones, volcanic craters, and lava flows are numerous in these ranges.

WATER RESOURCES

As might be expected for a country of such vast size, Russian water resources are enormous. Its territory contains some of the world's longest rivers and largest lakes. Hydrological potentials, however, are not equally distributed. While more than two million rivers flow through Russia, some areas remain parched during summer months when water is needed for agricultural purposes in particular. When lakes are included, the number of

Located in southern Siberia, Lake Baikal is the oldest (25 million years) and deepest (more than 5,000 feet, or 1,524 meters) lake in the world. In addition, it has the largest surface area of any lake in Asia, with a length of 395 miles (636 kilometers) and a width of 50 miles (81 kilometers).

water bodies climbs to more than six million. Lakes and rivers are unevenly distributed because of the uneven distribution of precipitation. A majority of rain falls during a few short months while snow accumulates during the long winter season. The largest amount of runoff occurs with spring snowmelt, which accounts for about two-thirds of the cumulative runoff.

Water resources do not correspond to the distribution of human settlement need. Whereas the majority of Russians live west of the Ural Mountains, two-thirds of the available fresh-water is located east of this dividing range. Additionally, in European Russia, decades of heavy industrialization and urban-ization contributed to a decrease in water quality for individual and commercial use. Rivers discharge into several main bodies of water—the Arctic and Pacific oceans, and the Black, Caspian, and Baltic seas. In terms of volume, the largest recipient is the Arctic Ocean, into which flow waters of the Ob-Irtysh, Yenisey, and Lena rivers. Their watersheds cover most of Asiatic Russia. Lakes are scattered throughout the country, but most are found in northern areas. A majority of the lakes were formed during the Pleistocene (ice age) period (1.8 million to 10,000 years ago) as continental glaciers advanced and retreated across the land. Both glacial scour and the pressure exerted on Earth's crust by the mass of glacial ice formed concave features on Earth's sur-face that became filled with water. Another kind of lake, a reser-voir, is man-made; that is, those artificial bodies of water are created by humans to fulfill certain purposes such as providing water for irrigation.

ENVIRONMENTAL CONCERNS AND PRESERVATION

The need to preserve the natural environment is not equally recognized by all people. In some countries, tall chimneys belching choking black smoke are regarded as symbols of progress, rather than contributors to environmental degrada-tion. Economic well-being is important to every country and its people. Simply stated, people need to feed families on a day-to-day basis, rather than concerning themselves with their impact on future generations by damaging the environment. Only when a society becomes economically well-off does the idea of environmental preservation begin to gain widespread acceptance. During the Soviet era, the notion of becoming an industrial powerhouse was widespread, as was the resulting negative impact on the natural environment. Government-controlled factories polluted the atmosphere, soils, and water.

Clear-cutting of forests occurred throughout the country. One must not rush to judgment and assume that only Communist governments create large environmental damage. The United States and most European countries share a similar history of industrial development. Russians tend to view their land as having infinite natural resources and, because of its tremendous size, possessing an ability to heal man-made wounds. Today, a great need exists to clean up previous environmental mistakes. Unfortunately, few funds are available to support this vital task.

Industrial, urban, and agricultural water pollution has created a very serious health hazard at many sites in Russia. Large numbers of urban centers and industrial complexes do not have water treatment plants. Raw sewage is pumped into rivers, lakes, ponds, and seas. State-owned and -managed public utilities account for 50 percent of all untreated sewage. The legacy of the Chernobyl catastrophe still haunts Russians. Even though it happened in Ukraine, many Russian settlements were affected. The Chernobyl accident was one of the world's worst industrial disasters. It killed more than 30 people who were working in the plant. Nuclear fallout contaminated prime agricultural land in southwestern Russia. Health officials report that at least 2.65 million Russians today live in contaminated areas. They also report that 185,000 Russians were exposed to radiation during the cleanup operation in 1986.

Although Russia's current environmental condition calls for serious attention, it should not imply that Russians do not care about conditions where they live. In fact, the idea of environmental protection has officially existed there for many decades. For instance, nature conservation programs were started during tsarist times. The country's protected area is measured in tens of millions of acres. Because of Russia's size and climatic diversity, conservation areas include lands that are home to nearly all ecosystems. Reserves are present throughout Russia, from the Pacific coast to Europe and from the Arctic Ocean to the Caucasus Mountain ranges. They are home to fascinating plant and animal species of which many are endemic (exist only at that location). The first conservation area was formed around Lake Baikal where, for example, more than half of the animal species are endemic. The management system of protected areas is structured through several levels. It also includes national parks and specially protected reserves.

CHAPTER

3

Russia Through Time

GROWTH OF THE STATE
Moscovite Rus: 1147–1462

At the beginning of the Christian era, the Slavic people were divided into three large cultural groups in three distinct portions of eastern Europe. The West Slavs lived in what is now central and southern Poland; the Middle Slavs lived between the east slopes of the Carpathian Mountains and the Dnieper River; and the East Slavs lived in the Don River valley. The physical and cultural environments offered many opportunities for human survival, and population increased rapidly.

By A.D. 500, Slavs had followed the rivers and moved to the north, east, and west. At this time, there were Slavic settlements throughout what was once called European imperial Russia. Sedentary, scattered tribes of Finns also inhabited much of the area into which the Slavs migrated. Successive waves of nomadic tribes that moved from the east across the steppes into the area north of the Black Sea affected the lives of the Slav settlers only slightly. The nomads fought for pasture, control of trade routes, and the power to extract tribute from the peaceful Slavic farmers. There was some intermarriage. Slavs who lived in the "black earth" areas tilled the land. Those who lived in the mixed and deciduous forests hunted, gathered honey and mushrooms, and planted small fields in cleared forest areas. Those who lived in the southern margins of the steppe were herdsmen. The Slavs lived primarily along rivers and traveled principally by canoe; the nomads ruled the steppe.

The Slavs recognized the importance of rivers for transportation and commerce. They founded trade centers on all the major rivers. Rivers linked the Slavs to the Baltic region, central Asian commercial centers, and the Eastern Roman Empire, known also as the Byzantine Empire (in present-day Turkey). To protect important trade routes from steppe nomads, the Slavs employed bands of Scandinavian warriors to defend the Slavic trade centers. The Varangians, as they all were called, brought all Slavic cities under one rule and established a new state, Kievan Rus. Its capital, Kiev, was located on the Dnieper River. Kievan Rus became a center of wealth and prestige because of trade. It traded with the Baltic nations through Varangian contacts, with the Chinese and Arabs through nomadic groups, and with the Finnish tribes through political control. Kievan Rus emerged as a rich commercial empire. Knowledge of Kiev's wealth spread throughout Europe and Asia. In the early 1200s, a highly mobile army of Mongols invaded Kievan Rus. After sacking a number of border cities, the Mongols withdrew. In the spring of 1240, they returned; 150,000 Mongolian horsemen conquered and pillaged Kiev.

In 1147, Yuri Dolgoruky, meaning "Yuri with the long arm," founded the city of Moscow on a hill overlooking the Moskva

River. He built a wall around the hill on the river's bank. This *kreml*, or fort (the original "Kremlin"), became an important defensive position. Those princes who succeeded Dolgoruky gained control over the entire Moskva River, from its headwaters to its mouth. The third prince of Moscow, Ivan Kalita (or as he was called, "money bags"), increased his possessions. He bought some land and acquired more through numerous marriages. He had his children marry nobles who owned land. By peaceful methods, Ivan Kalita and his sons made Moscow more important in the eyes of the Slavs and Mongols.

Under the shrewd leadership of its princes, Moscow became a rich city. When the leaders of the Russian Orthodox Church moved to Moscow, the city became the focal point of eastern Slavic culture. The Mongols controlled the land, but the princes of Moscow collected the taxes for them. By the latter half of the thirteenth century, the Golden Horde (Mongol invaders) was beginning to weaken. The princes of Moscow were quick to grasp the significance of this fact. Prince Dmitry (1359–1389) led an army against the Mongols and fought a battle near the headwaters of the Don River. The Mongols were routed. Dmitry proved that, although the Mongols still controlled the land of the Slavs, they were no longer invincible. In 1462, Moscow gained absolute control over the strategic river transport network of north and central Russia.

Moscovite Russia: 1463–1598

In 1463, the principality of Moscow was almost a solid block of territory. It included the upper Volga River, the Moskva River, the Oka River, portions of the Northern Dvina River in the north, and the Don River to the south. It extended to the Tatar city of Kazan in the east. Ivan III, the Great (1462–1505), captured the city-state of Novgorod in 1471 and tripled the size of his realm. He also ended Mongol control of Moscow in 1480. Although he won few military victories, Ivan ended nearly two and a half centuries of Mongol rule. Free of the Golden Horde, this principality became Moscovite Russia—a nation-state.

When Ivan III's wife died, he married Sophia, the orphaned niece of the last Byzantine emperor. Sophia was an intelligent, ambitious woman. She urged Ivan III to claim religious leadership of the Orthodox world. He took her advice, and Moscow became the "Third Rome." Ivan III declared himself "Tsar of all Rus" (Caesar of all Russians) and added the two-headed Byzantine eagle to the state crest and seal. His son, Vasily III (1505–1533), added more land to Russia, bringing all the "Great Russian" people under one rule.

As a three-year-old boy, Ivan IV, the Terrible (1533–1594), inherited Russia's "size" problem. His mother ruled in Ivan's name until she was poisoned in 1538. Ivan had himself crowned Tsar in 1547. He added the middle and lower Volga River basin and portions of the Ural Mountains and western Siberia to Russia; however, his attempts to capture the Baltic region failed miserably.

Deprived of family affection and denied the right to rule until he was 14, Ivan became ruthless. When he became the first official tsar of Russia in 1547, he reduced the influence of the Russian nobles. He prevented Russia from becoming a "constitutional monarchy." His reign was plagued by administrative disorder. The mad terror Ivan inflicted on his people doomed Russia to more troubles even after his death.

When Ivan the Terrible died in 1584, the throne passed to his simpleminded son Fyodor. Fyodor's only interest was the church. He especially enjoyed tolling church bells. Fyodor's brother-in-law, Boris Godunov, administered the nation for him. With Fyodor's death in 1598, the Rurik dynasty ended. Boris Godunov was elected tsar. Boris had been selected to begin the transition to a new dynasty. The deep-seated social unrest that followed Fyodor's death is called the "Time of Troubles."

Ivan IV, better known as Ivan the Terrible, ruled Russia from 1547 to 1584 and was the country's first proclaimed tsar. During his reign, Ivan centralized the government and initiated Russia's eastward expansion, conquering Kazan (present-day Tatarstan), Astrakhan (the delta region of the Volga River), and Siberia.

Romanov Russia: 1599–1689

Russia had just passed through the most difficult period in its history. It had been more painful than the 1917 revolution, the civil war, and the breakup of the Soviet Union would be centuries later. Plundering Cossacks had ravaged the lands. Native armies pillaged the countryside. Whole regions had been depopulated. Year after year, crops were destroyed. Towns were deserted. Men, women, and children had died horrible deaths. The reign of Ivan the Terrible and the Time of Troubles left Russia several generations behind western Europe intellectually and technically. The loss of territory also continued. The Swedes occupied Russian towns in the Baltic area, and took control of Novgorod. The Poles occupied western Russia and captured Smolensk. The Cossacks captured Samaria and Kazan. The first Romanov leader, Tsar Michael, began his reign in 1613.

Michael's first concern was to restore internal order, trade, and agriculture. He eased the threat from the Cossacks who lived in the southeast and made peace with Poland. Tsar Michael died in 1645. His successor, Alexis (1645–1676), incorporated Ukraine into Russia. With the help of the Zaporozhian Cossacks, the Russian Army captured much of Lithuania, recaptured Smolensk and the lands to the east of the Dnieper River, and recaptured Astrakhan at the mouth of the Volga River. Russia expanded very rapidly to the east, following the Steppe "road," the vast, flat, easy-to-cross steppe grasslands. Russians settled Okhotsk on the Pacific Ocean in 1649. In 1652, Irkutsk was founded, and a fort on the Amur River was constructed. That fort became the modern city of Khabarovsk. Upon his death in 1676, Alexis was succeeded by his 14-year-old, invalid son, Fyodor III (1676–1682), who reigned only six years. Alexis's two young sons—Ivan V and Peter I—succeeded Fyodor. Sophia, Ivan's sister, served as regent for them. In 1689, Peter I, the Great, deposed her.

Peter the Great's Russia: 1690–1725

Peter the Great developed a deep interest in boats from the Dutch sea captains he hired to handle Russian commercial interests. He became determined to give Russia a port on the Gulf of Finland and a port on the Black Sea. As part of this plan, Peter captured the Turkish stronghold of Azov at the mouth of the Dnieper River and built a naval base on the Sea of Azov. However, he had to give up Azov to the Turks when he became deeply involved in a 21-year war with Sweden. After a series of bitter losses to the Swedish king, Peter the Great eventually defeated the Swedes, and Russia became the dominant power in northern Europe.

One of Peter's greatest achievements was the founding of St. Petersburg in 1703. This city, at the head of the Gulf of Finland, deep in Swedish territory, took a decade to build. Determined that St. Petersburg would not be subject to fires like those that often ravaged Moscow, he instructed builders to make houses of stone. In 1714, Peter ordered the Senate to move to St. Petersburg. Foreign visitors to St. Petersburg that year considered the planned city one of the wonders of the modern world. Peter the Great's new capital was his "window on Europe."

Romanov Succesion: 1726–1762

From 1726 to 1762, the succession to the Russian throne was hopelessly confused. Peter the Great's decision to allow the current ruler to choose his or her own heir had brought many poor rulers to power. This period includes the reigns of Catherine I, Peter II, Anna, Ivan VI, Elizabeth, and Peter III. With the exception of Empress Elizabeth, many Russian leaders showed little interest in directing the affairs of state. During this period, the serfs (peasants who are tied to the land they work) lost the last shreds of the freedom that Peter the Great had given them.

Catherine the Great's Russia: 1762–1796

With the ascension of Catherine II ("The Great"), a true leader came to the throne. Catherine considered herself the executor of Peter the Great's reforms. Her greatest achievements were in adding territory and people of different cultural groups to Russia's empire. She directed two wars against the Turks, extending the Russian border to the Black Sea. Her troops occupied the Crimean Peninsula in 1783, followed by Odessa on the Black Sea in 1789. The western border of Russia was established along the Dniester River in Ukraine. Catherine instigated three partitions of Poland and by 1795, Poland was no longer an independent country. The period between 1796 and 1801, when Russia was ruled by Paul I, the son of Catherine, was one of political unrest.

Reform and Autocracy: 1801–1876

Tsar Alexander I, leader of the European response against French dictator Napoleon Bonaparte, has been called the "savior of Europe" and the "reformer of Russia." Alexander's reign began with the great hope of providing relief for the common Russian people. It ended in frustration and revolt. His sincere early efforts to resolve Russia's internal problems were diverted so he could work to curb the insatiable ambition of Napoleon. After a series of battles, Alexander and Napoleon agreed to peace at Tilsit (now Sovetsk, in western Russia) in 1807. Napoleon agreed to assist the tsar in "liberating" the Balkans, and gave Bessarabia (Moldova) to Alexander. Napoleon also encouraged Alexander to seize Finland in 1809. Alexander demanded control over the Bosporus Strait (the outlet of the Black Sea controlled by Turkey). He did not gain this prize, however. Alexander had expanded Russian influences into the Caucasus region and central Asia in hope of gaining control of the Ottoman Empire. Alexander captured Tiflis (Tbilisi) in 1801 and Baku in 1806 prior to the Treaty of Tilsit. Still unsatisfied, Napoleon ordered a 600,000-man French army to invade Russia in 1812. Napoleon captured Moscow, but lost the war because of the brutal Russian winter and the Russians' "scorched earth" policy. Alexander rode into Paris, France, at the head of his troops on March 31, 1814. Russia gained the Grand Duchy of Warsaw (Poland) as a result of the Vienna Settlement of 1815.

Exhausted from the demands of government, Alexander I died in December 1825. Soon after his death, a revolt by army officers and nobles who were called the "Decembrists" failed. Hopes of reforming Russia died with them. Nicholas I, who succeeded Alexander I, resisted all attempts at social reform. He used censorship and repression to stifle independent thought. Determined to play a leading role among the powers of the world, and in need of cotton for Moscow's textile industry, Russian troops moved into central Asia and captured Tashkent (in Uzbekistan) in 1875. To secure eastern Siberia and a Russian presence on the Pacific Ocean, all Amur River provinces were annexed and the city of Vladivostok was founded in 1860.

Revolutionary and Soviet Russia: 1877–1945

Internal unrest and national strikes presented great challenges for the tsars. The people wanted a stronger voice in national government. Between 1877 and 1917, the tsarist government battled a succession of progressive and revolutionary parties. Eventually, extremists overpowered the moderates and murdered Tsar Nicholas II. Then, empire builders pushed back the frontier in southeastern Siberia and in central Asia. Still, many problems plagued rural Russia. Good farmland was scarce. The serfs were emancipated by Tsar Alexander II in 1861, which had created economic costs. Transportation was poor. Nonetheless, industrial expansion was tremendous. At the end of the century, there were more than 1,700 successful corporations in Russia. Railroad construction, begun dramatically by Nicholas I, proceeded at a fast pace during the last decades of the nineteenth century. The most remarkable achievement of this period was the construction of the Trans-Siberian Railroad. It enabled Russia to gain influence in Manchuria and parts of northern China.

In 1894, Nicholas II assumed the throne. Under his rule, Russia's economy continued to grow. By the turn of the twentieth

Nicholas II was the last Russian tsar and reigned from 1894 to 1917, when he was forced to abdicate the throne by Communist revolutionaries known as Bolsheviks. Pictured here are Nicholas and his family. Bottom row, left to right: Princess Olga, Tsar Nicholas, Princess Anastasia, Prince Alexei, and Princess Tatiana; top row, left to right: Princess Maria and Empress Alexandra.

century, Russia ranked fourth in the world in iron smelting. However, the Russo-Japanese War of 1904–05 resulted in the defeat of the Russian Army. The southern half of Sakhalin Island was lost to Japan. The coming years would dramatically reduce those holdings.

Urban and rural unrest in Russia was triggered by the defeat in the Russo-Japanese War, and led to a revolution in

1905. Nicholas II granted some concessions to the people. Before the war in 1904, Russian territory had reached its greatest extent. World War I and events during and after the 1917 Russian Revolution caused Russia to lose some of its European territorial possessions. Finland, Estonia, Latvia, and Lithuania gained their independence. Romania claimed Bessarabia. The Soviet Union, however, soon regained the lost territory. As a victor in World War II, the Soviet Union acquired approximately 200,000 square miles (517,998 square kilometers) of land, mainly along its western border. By the end of 1945, the Soviet Union contained 8,606,300 square miles (22,290,214 square kilometers)—one-sixth of the earth's total land surface.

The Soviet Union, Russia, and the Independent Nations of the Former Soviet Union: 1945–Present

The Russian Revolution of 1917 launched the largest political and social experiment ever undertaken—the formation of the Soviet Union. Under the direction of the Communist Party, there was tremendous economic growth in the 1930s. With victory over the German Army in World War II, the Soviet Union became second in power only to the United States.

Following World War II, the Soviet Union regained most of the territory that had been a part of imperial Russia before 1913. The three Baltic republics—Estonia, Latvia, and Lithuania—were brought under Soviet control. Portions of eastern Poland, Moldova, and Bessarabia were seized from Romania. In addition, the northern part of East Prussia (now Kaliningrad, a small piece of Russian territory facing the Baltic Sea, between present-day Poland and Lithuania) fell under Russian rule for the first time. So did the Czechoslovakian province of Ruthenia (the "toe" of Czechoslovakia). Sakhalin and the Kuril Islands in the Far East were retaken from Japan. A small portion of the Mongolian Peoples' Republic, Tuva, was also annexed to the Soviet Union. The biggest changes in the nation's frontiers took place in the west. Soviet leaders considered that region a "danger zone," because two German invasions had already occurred there in the twentieth century.

In December 1991, the Commonwealth of Independent States (CIS) replaced the Soviet Union. Today, of all the former Soviet territories, only the Baltic states have not joined and perhaps never will. The CIS has a population of 280 million people and an area of 8.5 million square miles (13.7 million square kilometers). Tumultuous political antagonisms continue within many of the new nations. There, constant political turmoil is due to fragmented opposition groups, old-style Communist Party organizations, and the economic legacy of 70 years of failed central planning. Ongoing economic reforms within Russia will be critical to the future of all the new CIS nations.

4

People and Culture

POPULATION CHARACTERISTICS AND TRENDS

In the first half of the twentieth century, imperial Russia was transformed from a backward but powerful multiethnic nation into a major world superpower. Yet, from October 1917 until the death of Soviet leader Joseph Stalin in 1953, the people of the Soviet Union experienced one catastrophe after another. Millions of Russian soldiers died during World War I. At least 2 million people were killed in the Russian Civil War of 1919–1921. More than 3 million died between 1917 and 1923 in epidemics of cholera and typhus. A famine in 1921–1922 killed at least 9 million people. Another 5 million died during the forced collectivization of agriculture and the elimination of the kulaks (prosperous private farmers) in the early 1930s. A second major famine followed the horrors of forced collectivization in 1932–1934, when at least 9 million people died. Stalin's purges of the Communist Party and the rigors of concentration camps led to the deaths of 5 million people. Direct war-related deaths during World War II totaled more than 20 million. In 1946–1947, the Great Ukrainian Famine led to the loss of nearly 5 million Soviet citizens. Some demographers believe that the nation's 1989 census figure of 289 million would have been 200 to 250 million higher had the country been peaceful and wisely governed over the years.

Following Stalin's death, the Soviet Union went through a period of rapid population growth, followed by a decline. World War II left the nation with a great deficit of males. The process of balancing this abnormal sex distribution was slow. In 1950, there were 80 males for every 100 females. By 1970, this ratio had improved to 86 males per 100 females. In 1989, the ratio was 90 males per 100 females. These figures are still far from the 95–99 males per 100 females in populations with normal growth. In 1959, the number of females exceeded the number of males by 20.7 million. Thirty years later, this imbalance had been reduced to 15.7 million. Females begin to outnumber the males after the age of 40. Since migration into the Soviet Union was negligible, population increases since the end of World War II were determined by births and deaths. During the 10 years between 1979 and 1989, the Soviet Union's population increased by 24.3 million, or 9.3 percent.

The 1989 census showed the same regional shifts noted in 1959. One trend was the shift of the country's population center from west to east. This change was caused by high rates of natural increase in the central Asian republics and in Azerbaijan. Another long-term trend was the movement of many people from the western and central areas of European Russia to the southern republics. This led to serious regional imbalances in manpower. Young men continued to migrate from rural areas to cities. Growth in urban population was very high in central Asia, Azerbaijan, and Armenia. Here, urban growth resulted from high rates of both natural increase and immigration. The traditionally agricultural republics of Lithuania,

Belarus, and Moldova experienced massive rural-to-urban migration.

Urban population increased by 24.3 million between 1979 and 1989. Natural increase added 13.7 million people. Another 10.6 million migrated to urban areas. Rural population decreased by 900,000. At the same time, growing rural communities were reclassified as urban. In 1959, only three cities—Moscow, Leningrad, and Kiev—had more than one million inhabitants. By 1970, 10 cities exceeded the one-million mark. In 1989, there were 24 cities of one million or more. The number of cities with populations of 100,000 to 500,000 grew by 9 percent. The number of cities of between 500,000 and one million people increased by 18 percent. Population increases, both urban and rural, were not uniform. Most of the overall population growth took place in central Asia. The central Asian republics had a strong tradition of large families. There are many reasons these figures have not changed for decades, including the social structure of village life, the low level of education, and the reduction in infant mortality. Many Soviet demographers believed that high population growth reduced the quality of life; consequently, they strengthened family planning services in these areas.

The Russian Federation (Russia) is the largest post-Soviet nation. It contains more than 75 percent of the territory, but only half of the population of the former Soviet Union. Russia remains the world's largest country. With approximately 143 million people, Russia today has the world's sixth-largest population.

Russia's population growth rate is negligible. In some years, it is negative. For example, the estimated growth rate for 2001 was -0.35 percent, while five years later it still remained practically unchanged at -0.37 percent. Birthrates are very low, between 9 and 10 for every 1,000 people. Death rates are relatively high, at 13 to 15 per 1,000. The net migration rate is slightly more than one migrant per 1,000 people. Life expectancy in Russia has dropped drastically in the past decade. This reduction is the result of harsh economic conditions and poor medical care. Estimated male life expectancy has fallen to 60.45 years, the levels of many less developed countries. Female life expectancy is only 74 years. In the mid-1960s, life expectancy was 67 years for males and 76 years for females. Life expectancy for Russian males is similar to what it was for American men in the early 1940s. Russian females compare with U.S. women in the late 1950s. Overall, Russia's population is roughly 60 percent of the population of the United States.

Socioeconomic reasons influencing population trends remain similar among all former Soviet republics, including Russia. Lack of adequate resources and government funding during the 1990s damaged, in particular, health-care systems. Although conditions are gradually improving, it will take some time for Russia to reach the health standards of developed countries. Low life expectancy is strongly influenced by the effects of Russia's high rate of alcoholism among males. Russians have always battled with problems relating to excessive drinking. Economic hardship that occurred in postindependence years further contributed to social imbalances. As seen elsewhere, Russians also battle various diseases such as tuberculosis, and recently HIV/AIDS has spread rapidly. Various projections put the number of infected Russians at around one million. This is an especially difficult disease to battle because of extremely expensive treatments and medications, which ordinary people are unable to afford. The problem of rapidly spreading AIDS poses a major concern not only to Russia, but also to the other former Soviet republics. Ukraine, for example, faces an AIDS crisis. Russia, however, faces another challenge. It may lose international funds for prevention of AIDS because of its recognition as a middle-income country due to rising revenue from high energy prices. Thus, the country may slide from the largest single recipient of foreign help for AIDS prevention to almost no help at all. On a positive note, Russia has well-educated health-care professionals who can reorganize the system once the government manages to provide adequate financial resources. That will stop the expansion of AIDS and other diseases, while increasing the quality of life, especially those in lower economic classes.

REGIONAL DISTRIBUTION OF POPULATION

Population distribution and redistribution in Russia has been managed by the government. Recently, it has been modified by the economic restructuring associated with the breakup of the Soviet Union. The population hub of imperial Russia was Moscow, which was the largest city in the Soviet Union. In 1724, Peter the Great ordered the first census taken in tsarist Russia. It covered only the European, or western, portion of the country. The last census taken by the Soviet government was in 1989. It was a complete census that provided much detail. Since the fall of the Soviet Union, Russian population data show great changes in density and internal migration. Parallel to the initial decline in population, there has been a continuous process of redistribution. People move from area to area. They leave the countryside for cities (rural-to-urban migration). At least 90 percent of Russia's population lives west of the Ural Mountains. Those who live east of the Urals are primarily found in a 50-mile (81-kilometer) band on either side of the Trans-Siberian Railroad. Others are scattered in isolated settlements throughout the tundra. The densest population is found in the Moscow region, around St. Petersburg and the rail corridor to Moscow, along the Volga River and its major tributaries, in the central section of the Ural Mountains, and in the region surrounding Novosibirsk. Similar to the United States, approximately 75 percent of the population resides in urban areas.

Originally, Slavic pioneers moved east from the northern slope of the Carpathian Mountains. They practiced slash-and-burn agriculture, without setting up permanent villages. As

Moscow is Russia's capital and largest city with a population of 10.4 million people. Approximately 75 percent of Russia's population resides in urban areas, and 13 of its cities have a population in excess of one million. This September 2005 photo of Tverskaya Street, in downtown Moscow, shows people celebrating the eight-hundred-fifty-eighth anniversary of the city's founding.

their population increased, the Slavs began to cluster together to avoid social isolation. They sought protection against marauding bands of nomads. The Mongol and Tatar invasions of the thirteenth century intensified the Slavic pattern of banding together for common defense. Village sites were selected primarily for defense. The Russian word for "city," *gorod*, originally meant "hill" or "hill fortress." Because land was so plentiful, there was no concept of private land ownership. Peasant farmers would journey out of their small villages to work communally owned fields. As rudimental transportation networks developed, trade increased. Regularity in the selection of settlement sites, village patterns, and settlement forms emerged. During the fourteenth and fifteenth centuries, villages in newly settled areas were platted (designed) by noble landowners, church administrators, or tsarist administrators. Serfdom provided a means of government control. It kept peasant farmers from leaving rural villages and towns. At the same time, it slowed rural and small-town economic and social development until it was abolished in 1861.

Rural settlement patterns in the period of Russian expansion to the tundra and taiga regions reflected the people's predominant economic activities, including hunting, fur trapping, and fishing. Permanent settlement sites were chosen at confluences (the joining) of streams, in river valleys above flood level, and on southern-facing slopes. Breaks in navigation or waterfalls along a river were often selected for a settlement. Natural harbors on lakeshores or on major bodies of water were other favored sites.

South of the tundra and taiga, mixed and deciduous forests covered the glaciated plains. In this region, villages and towns were established on small hills or mounds. The southern-facing slopes were warmer in winter and drier in summer, enabling the people to grow a greater range of crops. As in the far north, settlers favored sites at the confluence of streams or rivers and at easily defended places. Many larger towns and small cities grew around a fort, or *kremlin*. Examples include Moscow, Kazan, Tver, and Novgorod. Kremlins were natural defense positions, surrounded by walls and ditches (moats). Arsenals, palaces, churches, and commercial enterprises were built within the kremlin so that life could continue as normally as possible in time of siege.

South of the mixed and deciduous forest regions, the wooded steppe and steppe dominate the landscape. Here, settlers preferred to establish villages on the highest bank of a river, at a confluence of rivers or streams, or near a natural ford (a place where a river can easily be crossed because of shallow water). At Volgograd, the original settlements eventually merged into large towns. The settlements became a city situated on high western bluffs overlooking the river.

Farthest south, in the semidesert and desert regions, early settlements were located where there was adequate water. Places where a defensible position existed were also favorable sites.

Initially, the emancipation of the serfs within imperial Russia in 1861 had little effect on rural settlement patterns. Aristocratic landowners and the Russian Orthodox Church were required to give the peasants land. However, the land was assigned to villages for communal administration, and land payment had to be made to the tsar for land received from the nobles. Change finally came with the land reforms of 1905–1906. These reforms allowed farmers to acquire and live on their own farmland outside of villages. Within 10 years, one-fourth of all rural dwellers left the rural villages (called "communes"). Single-family homesteads became the main form of settlement in western Ukraine and the Baltic area.

In the 1930s, the Soviet government attempted to consolidate all private farms. Small villages were to be merged into larger ones in an attempt to gain greater control over food supplies for urban dwellers. The state-directed process of eliminating small villages continued through the 1960s and 1970s. They created large rural population centers. Today, rural villages in Russia range in size from a few households to more than 20,000 inhabitants.

The site selection and economic base for the major cities of the Soviet Union were determined in the last half-century of tsarist rule. This was the period of rapid urban growth, railroad building, industrial expansion, and international trade. In the mid-nineteenth century, there were only two cities with populations in excess of 100,000 people. By 1913, there were 30. Moscow and St. Petersburg both doubled their populations in this time. New port and industrial cities in Russia and Ukraine grew in size and economic importance. Odessa, Rostov-on-Don, and Yuzovka (Donetsk) were three of these.

In 1926, one out of five Russians lived in an urban area. By 1989, two out of every three were urban dwellers. Soviet urban centers had to absorb more than 150 million people in a little more than 60 years. Massive industrial growth in the 1930s, followed by World War II, led to a shortage of urban housing. Many of the Soviet Union's largest cities and their buildings were severely damaged or destroyed in the war.

The rapid growth of cities between 1926 and 1939 has never been equaled elsewhere before or since. Cities of all sizes—small, medium, and large—more than doubled. Moscow's population increased by 1.7 million in one decade.

This rapid urban growth created problems, however. Quality of life suffered. There were shortages of housing, goods, and services. Nowhere were the problems more severe than in the many newly built cities.

Communist leaders believed they had to urbanize in order to industrialize the Soviet Union as quickly as possible. Instead of gradual industrial development, a series of five-year plans set bold goals. Villages were to become cities. Small handicraft units and factories were to become huge industrial complexes.

The fastest-growing cities were in regions with the greatest industrial growth. By 1939, most industrial cities had tripled their populations. In 1939, urban centers of 100,000 or more were centers of industry, transportation, or trade. Some were also centers of political administration. After World War II, the cities took on more functions. Some became centers for education and training. Others added research and development facilities. Resort and recreation areas appeared. However, manufacturing became even more important than it had been before the war.

During World War II, the German Army destroyed 1,700 urban centers. Twenty-five million people were left homeless. They needed employment, as well as food and housing. The Soviet government devised a crash program to rebuild the ruined cities. Construction was simplified and the least-expensive materials were used. As a result, style and quality suffered.

Prefabricated, reinforced concrete slabs were assembled into apartment buildings. Quality and diversity were sacrificed to increase quantity. Housing, transportation, and pollution problems abounded. Still, Soviet cities continued to grow, and more new cities were founded. By 1989, the Soviet Union was a land of great cities. It contained 24 cities with more than one million inhabitants each. More than 50 cities had populations of more than half a million. No other country had as many cities with so many residents as the Soviet Union at the time it dissolved. Today, Russia is still predominantly an urban nation.

ETHNIC GROUPS

Beginning at the pivotal point of Moscow, Russian influence expanded continuously outward. In just more than 500 years (from 1462 to 1991), it spread to cover more than one-third of Europe and nearly half of Asia. The tsars and then the Soviet commissars brought much territory and many ethnic groups under their control. They governed large numbers of people from diverse backgrounds. Russian social scientists believed that the key feature of nationality was the possession of a common language, so they classified people into linguistic groupings. The 1926 Soviet census counted 169 nationalities. The 1989 census listed 104. The political framework outlined in the Soviet constitution was based largely on ethnic lines. Each of the 15 Soviet republics was named after its largest nationality group. Some large republics had special administrative regions for people from ethnic minorities.

The Slavic Peoples

Slavs are the dominant ethnic group within Russia and within the new CIS. Historically, three main Slavic groups have been recognized. These groups have little in common beyond their similar origin and linguistic connections. Different historical experiences have produced dissimilar cultural and physical characteristics. For example, most Russians are believed to be taller than Ukrainians and Belarusians. Slavs are generally fair-skinned. Their hair is usually wavy and ranges in color from blond to red to brown. In fact, physical characteristics may have played a role in naming the three major Slavic ethnic groups: Russians (Great Russians), Ukrainians (Little Russians), and Belarusians (White Russians).

Russians

Russians have lived in and around Moscow, Vladimir, and Suzdal for thousands of years. Intermarriage with other ethnic groups was common among them. As a result, Scandinavian and Mongolian racial features and culture have had an impact on Russians.

The Russians were the great pioneers who moved out of their core area around Moscow into all areas of imperial Russia, and later, the Soviet Union. Early in their history, they survived and triumphed over invading tribes, including the Mongols, Tatars, Swedes, Germans, and even the Poles. In recent history, the Russians overcame major invasions by the Turks, French, and Germans.

Many factors have unified the Russians. First, they were united by their adoption of Greek Orthodox Christianity. Later, tsarism and Communism held them together. During the twentieth century, fear of the Germans and distrust of the United States and Western European powers united them. Today, they share their traditional love for the land ("Mother Russia," as they call it) and a desire to become a partner of the United States in global diplomacy.

In 1989, more than 145 million Russians lived throughout all the nations of the former Soviet Union. Most Russians who live in the former Soviet republics consider Russia their mother country. Ukraine and Kazakhstan host the largest groups of ethnic Russians outside of Russia. Moscow remains their cultural capital. As the country's name implies, Russians dominate the Russian Federation—they made up more than 80 percent of the total 1989 population, a number that holds today.

Shortly before the Soviet Union collapsed in 1991, there were more than 4 million Ukrainians living in Russia. Today, their numbers remain steady—more than 4.3 million Ukrainians call Russia home, approximately 47 percent of whom live in the Kuban region of southwestern Russia. Here, a Ukrainian woman sells meat to a Russian woman at a market in Moscow.

Ukrainians

When the census was taken in 1989, it reported that more than 4 million Ukrainians were living in the Russian Federation. Although at least 3 percent of the total population of the Russian Federation is Ukrainian, the Ukrainian cultural hearth is western Ukraine and Kiev. Kiev, because of its historical significance, is considered the "mother" of all Slavic cities.

Ukrainians were deeply impacted, both culturally and racially, by contact with the Turks, Mongols, and Tatars in their early history. Later, Lithuanians and Poles also made an imprint. Most Ukrainians are Orthodox Christians, but in western portions of Ukraine, many are Roman Catholic or Uniate Christians. Kiev, one of the most beautiful cities in

Europe, has a large Russian minority. The majority of ethnic Russians reside in Ukraine's eastern regions adjacent to Russia.

Belarusians

Scandinavians, Lithuanians, and Poles have greatly influenced the Belarusians, but the isolation afforded by the swamps and thick forests of Belarus have helped them retain their cultural heritage. Orthodox Christianity and Roman Catholicism are the two major religious denominations of Belarus. The 1989 census reported that more than one million Belarusians were living in the Russian Federation.

Unfortunately, a major invasion route from the west to Moscow crosses Belarusian land. The people who dwelled along this route have suffered terribly at the hands of foreign soldiers. During World War II, the German Army killed 10 percent of the Belarusian people.

Turkic and Related Peoples

Turkic peoples form the second-largest ethnic group within Russia and the CIS. They comprise at least 10 percent of all those who live within the borders of Russia. These peoples are of central Asian origin. Most are Muslims (followers of Islam). Like other nomadic pastoralists and sedentary oasis farmers in dry central Asia, Turkic peoples spread out in several directions from their homelands. Traveling through northern Iran around the southern shore of the Caspian Sea, some migrated into the eastern Caucasus region and into Turkey. Today, these people are called Azeris or Azerbaijanis.

Some Turkic peoples, such as Bashkirs, Tatars, and Chuvash, migrated to the northwest into the area between the Volga River and the southern Ural Mountains. Others migrated northeastward into Siberia. There, the Khakass, Altays, Trevinians, and Yakuts were able to survive in isolation.

Almost all of these groups speak a Turkic language. Their physical characteristics, though, are as diverse as where they live. Despite this fact, in Russian scientific literature, they have been described as generally having tan skin, broad and round heads, straight black hair, and Mongolian eyes. Heights vary among Turkic groups.

Various Turkic and related peoples today live in the area between the Volga River bend and the Ural Mountains. The Tatars, Bashkirs, and Chuvash live in a transition area between the deciduous forest zone and the forest steppe. For centuries, those who lived in the steppe zone pastured their sheep and horses on the rich steppe grasses. They grew crops in the rich chernozem soils that characterize this zone. Rich deposits of oil and economically significant minerals lie beneath these deciduous forests and grasslands.

The Chechens and Ingush live in a beautiful section of the northern Caucasus Mountains. Grozney, their capital, is an oil-refining center that serves a rich oil-production region in the north Caucasus foothills and plains.

Tatars, Bashkirs, and Chuvash fought with the Soviets in the Red (Soviet) Army during World War II. Chechens and Ingush, on the other hand, were accused of treasonable collaboration with the Germans. Many were deported from their homeland. After Stalin's death, the Chechen-Ingush administrative unit was restored and the people were permitted to return home. Buryat Mongols live in eastern Siberia around Lake Baikal. A native Siberian people, they had been conquered by the Russians in the early 1700s. They are Buddhists. Kalmyk Mongols live on the northwest shore of the Caspian Sea. A nomadic people, they had migrated from western China in the early 1600s.

Other Ethnic Groups

Finno-Ugrian people were living in what is now Russia when the Slavic people migrated eastward from the north slopes of the Carpathian Mountains in southern Poland. As their name illustrates, these people are relatives to Finns and Hungarians.

Modern Finno-Ugrians in Russia include the Mordovinians, Udmurts, and Maris of the Volga River bend area. They also include the Komis of northeastern European Russia and the Karelians, who live in northwestern Russia, along the Finnish border. Although few in number (about 180,000 in the 1989 census), Finno-Ugrian, Altaic, and Palaeoasiatic groups are the primary inhabitants of northern Siberia. The Chukchis and Koryakis inhabit northeastern Siberia. Inuits (Eskimosy) and Aleuts live on the coastal fringe of far eastern Siberia.

Jews and Germans are also numerically important. Jews migrated into imperial Russia hundreds of years before the Russian Revolution of 1917. They were fleeing persecution in western Europe. Catherine the Great invited Germans into the country to help settle the steppe region of southwestern Russia. Russian Germans were regarded as expert farmers and productive citizens, although they were often perceived as foreigners even after several generations lived on Russian soil. Toward the end of the nineteenth century and the beginning of the twentieth many of them left Russia and settled very successfully in the Northern Plains region of the United States and Canada's Prairie Provinces.

Since the breakup of the Soviet Union, there has been an out-migration of minorities. Inhabitants who owed their ethnic allegiance to another independent nation of the former Soviet Union left Russia. Russians living in other places returned to the Russian Federation. Large numbers of Jews, Germans, Ukrainians, and Belarusians migrated.

RELIGION

Russian society has always depended upon a common set of beliefs to blend together its diverse members. These beliefs had a place of origin and entry into Russia, routes of diffusion, and patterns of distribution. Religions of Russia vary greatly, and include beliefs in one God, many gods, ancestor worship, forest glade spirits, magic, and idol worship. The majority of those who live in the Russian Federation, however, are Christians of the Russian Orthodox tradition or Sunni Muslims. Ideologies and formalized religions stress distinct attitudes toward life. They strongly influenced the development of Russian society. In Russia, almost all religions and ideologies interact with political, social, and economic activities. Russia was, is, and will probably always be a nation of deeply religious people.

The Russian Orthodox Church is the religious denomination that has the largest membership within the Russian Federation. Orthodox beliefs are based on the Bible and tradition. Decrees of church councils and the writings of early church leaders established the authority of church doctrines. Daily church services rely on the Bible, especially the book of Psalms. Orthodox churches are richly decorated with religious art. Icons (holy images) are an essential part of Orthodox tradition. These ornate and revered images have long served to stimulate faith and piety in worshipers. The Russian Orthodox Church has seven major sacraments. In Russia, there are thousands of Orthodox churches—both large and small—made of wood and stone. Many are considered architectural masterpieces.

Islam, which means "submission to God," is primarily the religion of Turkic and related peoples. Based upon the teachings of Muhammad, the keystone of Islamic doctrine is, "There is no God but Allah." The *Qur'an* (Koran) is the sacred book of the Muslims. Each Muslim must observe the "five pillars" of the faith, which include a month of fasting, almsgiving, and a pilgrimage to Mecca, Islam's holiest city. The majority of Russian Muslims follow the Sunni doctrine of Islam. They live mainly along the Volga River and in the area between the Volga River and the Ural Mountains. There are thousands of mosques in the Russian Federation.

Many other religious groups are found in the Russian Federation. These include the Roman Catholic Church, Evangelical

Approximately 15 to 20 percent of Russians are practitioners of the Russian Orthodox religion. Pictured here is St. Basil's Cathedral in Moscow's Red Square. Built during the reign of Ivan IV in the mid-1500s, the cathedral is Moscow's most recognizable landmark.

Christian-Baptists, Buddhists, Seventh-Day Adventists, Molokans, Lutherans, Pentecostals, Assemblies of God, and Jehovah's Witnesses. More recently, missionary work of Protestant groups from the West, the United States in particular, has been quite active in Russia. These groups are involved in various social projects for the poor, but also in the spread of their own beliefs, thereby contributing to Russia's religious mosaic.

Most Russian members of the Catholic Church can be found in the European part of the former Soviet Union, especially in urban centers. Catholics live in Lithuania, western Ukraine, western Belarus, and southern Latvia. A doctrinal split between the Orthodox and Catholic churches restricted the spread of Catholicism into Russia. Nevertheless, beautiful Catholic churches were constructed in St. Petersburg, Moscow, and most large Russian cities. There are hundreds of active Catholic communities in Russia.

Judaism is distinguished by a commitment to the one God that Jews contend chose them in a solemn covenant. In imperial Russia, Jews were excluded from many occupations. The majority became traders, artisans, bankers, and commercial middlemen. It is estimated that 98 percent of Russian Jews today live in cities and towns. There are almost 200 active Jewish organizations in Russia. Since the creation of Israel, the number of Jews in Russia has declined, because many immigrated to the new Jewish state, a trend that continues today.

Evangelical Christian-Baptists are a fast-growing Christian denomination. There are at least 500,000 believers in Russia. They publish Bibles, books on the Gospels, calendars, and religious journals. Church services are performed in most of the major languages spoken in the Russian Federation.

Buddhism, as practiced in Russia, is of the Helukpa school (the "school of virtue"). It originated in Tibet. Most Buddhists live in the Buryat, Tuva, and the Kalmyk administrative regions of southern Siberia and north of the Caspian Sea. Ulan Ude, a beautiful city east of Lake Baikal in Siberia, is the center of Russian Buddhist activities.

There has been remarkable growth in the number and in the diversity of religious groups in Russia since 1991. Currently, there are more than 10,000 registered Russian Orthodox congregations. (Religious groups must register with the Justice Ministry. Groups that fail to do so cannot open bank accounts, rent property, or print religious documents.) There are more than 3,000 Muslim groups, almost 200 Jewish organizations, and nearly 200 Buddhist temples. There also has been a dramatic explosion of Protestant groups. These include approximately 3,000 Evangelical Christian-Baptist churches, 350 Jehovah's Witness branches, 200 Presbyterian congregations, and 500 other Protestant communities. Russia has never had such diversity in its religious groups. One of the main reasons for the religious renaissance is that now political authorities are not as concerned about religious issues as they were during the Communist era. Therefore, people are allowed to freely enjoy religion without any fear of government reprisal.

MIGRATION AND MOBILITY

Russia's population began to decline shortly after the breakup of the Soviet Union, even though it had been growing since World War II. The current socioeconomic transition Russia is experiencing accounts for most of this decline. Russian leaders are worried that the slow population growth could create labor shortages in areas of economic growth. It also could lead to uncontrolled internal migration. There are great differences in birth, death, and natural increase rates throughout Russia. In general, higher birth and natural increase rates are found in Siberia, the Far East, and in autonomous ethnic group regions. Economic problems and reduction of state financial incentives (higher wages) have led to an out-migration from northern and eastern Siberia, the Ural Mountain region, and the Far East. There is some in-migration in western Siberia, where oil fields are located. Internal out-migration in northern Russia, west of the Ural Mountains, is greatest in the Murmansk area and the Komi area. Reductions in military bases and closures of some economic activities have forced people to move south.

Since the fall of the Soviet Union, there has been massive in-migration from other post-Soviet republics. Almost 3 million Russians have moved back to their home country. In the early 1990s, many people of Russian ethnic origin felt some repercussions in former republics. In places like the Baltic states, Russians were relegated to second-class citizens. Politically motivated decisions established linguistic provisions that made Russian, once the official language to all, nonofficial. Many ethnic Russians, some of them living in these states for generations, decided to move to Russia, rather than lose their ethnic identity. Unfortunately for the new states, vast numbers of those who decided to leave for Russia were educated people who could otherwise contribute to the local economy.

The migration of so many people into Russia has placed great strains upon existing housing, social services, and public facilities. Russia also has experienced a large return of military personnel, who were required to leave post-Soviet republics and central European countries after the Soviet Union fell. The government has identified a number of areas of Russia as "reception regions" for migrants. Most are located in agricultural areas with a low population. However, most migrants prefer to move to large towns and cities in the central and southern portions of western Russia. Russia's traditional population distribution patterns have also been modified by an out-migration of more than 600,000 Russians to other countries of the world. Most of these people go to Germany, the United States, Canada, and Israel.

URBAN/RURAL CONTRASTS

Throughout the history of the Soviet Union, and particularly during the first Five-Year Plan, Russians migrated from rural areas to urban areas in search of jobs and better lives. Today, Russians in large urban areas have a higher standard of living than those from rural regions. They also have better medical and social services, better schools, more interesting jobs, and pay less in rent. Many state welfare benefits are unavailable in rural areas.

Approximately 75 percent of the population of Russia lives in urban areas. Soviet planners favored big cities. They provided more funds for them than for smaller cities (of less than 50,000 inhabitants) and rural areas. Many smaller Russian towns still have few social services, such as health care, schools, and shopping centers, and have relatively low standards of living.

In general, city dwellers in Russia today have to cope with numerous problems, almost all related to government neglect. There is an acute shortage of affordable housing. Overcrowded public transportation systems, poor health services, and antiquated systems of shopping are common. With the exception of Moscow, St. Petersburg, and other very big urban centers, little state money is available for urban improvement. Entrepreneurs (the "New Russian" business-people), who are making money from the growing capitalist economy, live well in the big cities. However, at the same time, large numbers of poor people and pensioners struggle to survive. They are victims of inflation and unemployment.

Russia, like the United States, is an urbanized society. Even so, approximately 25 percent of the nation's population still lives in rural areas. Collectivization of agriculture and incomes below poverty level have disrupted rural life since the early years of Soviet rule. Stalin's collectivization program forced farmers to give their land, animals, and farm implements to the state and work collectively with other farmers on large state-controlled or state-managed agricultural enterprises. Under Soviet rule, rural dwellers had the low status given to peasants. Many rural dwellers looked for any opportunity to leave the farms for towns and cities. Rural depopulation on an alarming scale plagued European Russia, Siberia, and the Far East. Those who remained in rural areas were generally elderly, very conservative, less educated, or not motivated to look for change. Since the breakup of the Soviet Union, rural Russia

Under Soviet rule, inhabitants of rural parts of Russia, such as these women who are tending to their sheep and cows, were forced to give up their land and livestock to the Communist government. During this period, Russia's rural population dropped significantly, because many people left in search of better opportunities.

has suffered from high inflation and low agricultural prices. There is little credit available for farm improvements and new equipment. State support for agricultural activities is limited. It is difficult to market farm products. High costs of fuel have also increased rural isolation. As a result, the quality of rural life is declining further. In many parts of rural Russia today, people live and work at subsistence levels similar to those in the early twentieth century.

RUSSIA'S FUTURE POPULATION

Prior to the breakup, the Soviet Union had one of the fastest-growing populations among the world's developed countries. Its annual population growth rate was approximately 0.9 percent, slightly lower than that of the United States. However, by the early 1990s, Russia's population began to decrease at a rate that alarmed government officials and economic planners. Low birthrates and higher death rates are caused by uncertainty, economic disruption, declines in health care, and dietary changes related to economic and social turmoil. For the first 40 years of its existence, the Soviet Union made remarkable improvements in the health conditions of its people. Since 1990, however, the gap in life expectancy between the United States and Russia has grown steadily wider. If the health sector in Russia is further neglected, the mortality rate will undoubtedly increase, and life expectancy will continue to decline. Birthrates in major Russian cities are at the lowest level they have been in decades. Russian couples' confidence in the future is so uncertain that many are not having children. Throughout Russia, in both rural and urban settings, there has been a marked change in childbearing patterns. Population projections for Russia assume that the recent trends of population decline will continue. Based on data from the Council on Europe and the Population Reference Bureau, Russia's population could decline from 148 million in 1990 to 140 million in 2010. This projection reflects the extreme demographic consequences following the Soviet Union's breakup. Concerned with demographic issues, the Russian government has acknowledged the need for serious changes. In his 2006 annual address to the nation, President Vladimir Putin asked Russians to improve the country's demographic picture. He offered financial incentives to couples with children, doubling the amount of aid for every subsequent child.

5

Government and Politics

TSARISM

The peoples of Russia have been governed by some of history's most oppressive and authoritarian political regimes. One family—the Romanovs—governed Russia's diverse ethnic and linguistic groups for more than 300 years. Initially elected by the noble gentry during the "Time of Troubles," the Romanovs developed a form of government called tsarism. The male who inherited the throne of imperial Russia was called a tsar, a title that comes from the word Caesar. A female ruler was called a tsarina. The first Romanov tsar was Michael. He began his reign in 1614. The last Romanov tsar, Nicholas II, was forced to give up his right to rule in 1917 and shortly later was executed together with other members of his family.

The tsarist regimes in general were centralized, self-centered dictatorships of the Romanov family and their wealthy noble supporters.

The Russian tsar or tsarina had uncontrolled and unlimited authority over all the inhabitants of imperial Russia. Over the span of 300 years, the tsars devised a governmental system that would ensure their authority and their survival. They enforced political obedience, which left many people disenfranchised and angry. Tsars varied in administrative skills and ruthlessness. In the decades prior to the 1917 Russian Revolution, tsars worked obsessively to find methods to unify their ethnically diverse empire and to reinforce their despotic rule. The program of "Russification" that they used included imposing Russian culture, including language and the Russian Orthodox religion, on non-Russian minorities. Opposition to the tsarist government became very intense during the late 1880s and early 1900s. Nicholas II was an ineffective leader. His failure to respond to his people's needs led to a revolution. Additional political unrest occurred after Russia suffered heavy loses in World War I in the conflict with Germany. The inability to counter German forces cost Russians hundreds of thousands of lives, which created destabilization and set the ground for revolution. The murder of Nicholas II and his family cleared the way for the establishment of a Communist dictatorship.

COMMUNIST DICTATORSHIP

Massive general strikes, hunger, and a loss of faith in Nicholas II led up to the Bolsheviks seizing control of Russia. Vladimir Lenin, the Communist Party leader, was a brilliant revolutionary. His leadership of the highly disciplined Communist Party, combined with the country-destroying events of 1917, enabled the Bolsheviks to overthrow the tsarist system. Immediately following their seizure of power, they established a government based upon Marxist ideology. Karl Marx, a German thinker and revolutionary, had written about how a Communist society might be created. He proposed a society that would have common ownership of all means of production and no social classes. In an ideal Communist society, there would be no want

Leading up to Nicholas II's abdication of the throne in March 1917, many Russians expressed their displeasure over Russia's sagging economy through massive strikes and rioting. However, once the Bolsheviks took control of the country, Russians took to the streets to celebrate the new government.

and no exploitation of working people. Lenin recognized, however, that Marx's model of a government system would have to be modified for use in Russia. Lenin replaced exploitative capitalism with a socialist economic system.

The Communist Party and the workers of former tsarist Russia would create the necessary preconditions for a true Communist society. The first step was to establish a dictatorship of socialist workers under the direction of a single political power—the Communist Party. The second step was to create a new centralized government that would bring all peoples together. The third step involved the elimination of differences based upon wealth, race, religion, and other sources of social conflict. In this step, the Communists did away with private property and nationalized all industrial and commercial activities. The fourth step was to formulate a national social security and national welfare system for all the people of Russia. Soviet Russia and, later, the Soviet Union were to be socialist states working toward pure Communism. They hoped to eventually achieve Marx's goal in which all work and benefits would be distributed "from each according to his ability, to each according to his needs." The fifth step was to formulate agencies within the government to rid society of those who would oppose Communism. To do this, the Communists created the dreaded secret police. Russia's new political system was brutal. It forced radical socioeconomic changes upon the country and its people.

After a period of deprivation, famine, and a civil war, Russia became the foundation for the Union of Soviet Socialist Republics. With three other republics, it formed the Soviet Union in 1922. The constitution of the Soviet Union recognized ethnic diversity. It provided for the creation of 16 union republics. A *soviet*, or council, would govern each of the union republics (which were later reduced in number to 15). According to the constitution, all political power was in the hands of the people. In reality, however, the Communist Party controlled the Soviet Union. The Supreme Soviet of the Soviet Union was similar to the Congress of the United States. All of its members were elected to four-year terms. The Supreme Soviet was divided into two houses. The Soviet of the Union, made up of deputies elected on the basis of population, was similar to the U.S. House of Representatives. Members of the Soviet of Nationalities were elected from ethnic groups. A Presidium of the Supreme Soviet conducted governmental operations between sessions of the two houses (the two Soviets). A Council of Ministers, or cabinet, was the highest executive body. The council chairman, or premier, was the actual head of the government. Dictators, such as Joseph Stalin and Nikita Khrushchev, held this position while they also headed the Communist Party.

Leaders of the Communist Party and the Soviet Union after Khrushchev (who was removed from power in 1964) attempted to ease the harshness of Soviet life. They tried to make the government more democratic. Despite their efforts, Leonid Brezhnev, Yuri Andropov, and Konstantin Chernenko were unable to overcome the internal problems that were causing economic stagnation. In 1985, Premier Mikhail Gorbachev recognized the weaknesses and flaws of Soviet society. He predicted that social upheaval would result unless the country took care of its internal problems. He introduced policies of "openness" (glasnost) and "restructuring" (perestroika) to reform the stagnant Soviet system. Rather than solve problems, these reforms actually disrupted economic life, disappointed the people, compromised the government, divided Soviet society, and weakened the Communist Party. All of these dramatic changes led the Soviet Union to collapse in 1991. After the breakup of the Soviet Union, the 15 constituent republics became independent nations. Because of its size, population, and natural wealth, Russia remained the most powerful of the ex-Soviet republics.

RUSSIA AFTER COMMUNISM

Most of Russia's people were skeptical about adopting a Western-style democracy in 1991. Russian president Boris Yeltsin warned the people that the country had more problems than a parliamentary democracy could resolve. He advocated instead a "presidential government." Keeping the old Soviet government model, Yeltsin attempted to reform Russian society. (The Russian Constitution, which had been rewritten in 1977, was amended in 1991 to create the office of president. However, it gave most governmental power to the Parliament.) Many of Yeltsin's actions were very undemocratic. He issued laws that exceeded his legal rights under the constitution. He bypassed the Russian Parliament because it was dominated by conservative Communist Party members who had been elected in 1989. To strengthen the presidency, in 1993, Yeltsin called for a new constitution and the

On May 7, 2000, Vladimir Putin (right) became president of Russia, succeeding Boris Yeltsin. The two are pictured here in the Kremlin on Putin's first day as acting president on December 31, 1999.

creation of a new Parliament. He suspended the existing constitution and announced elections for the State Duma and the Confederation Council (later renamed the Federation Council), the new Parliament. Members of both houses would be elected directly by voters for four-year terms. The people of Russia approved the new constitution, which created an executive-oriented parliamentary democracy that resembles the government of France. The 1993 constitution gives the president a great deal of power, but weakened the national legislature.

RUSSIA IN THE TWENTY-FIRST CENTURY

Vladimir Putin became the acting president of Russia on December 31, 1999, and president on May 7, 2000. His election sidelined proposals to reduce the president's power. The people supported the new constitution. They wanted to eliminate the decision-making stalemate between the president and Parliament. Conflicts between the executive and legislative branches of government had paralyzed the nation's economy to the detriment of society. Elected to a four-year term, Putin received 53 percent of the popular vote. The candidate who came in second won only 29 percent. Putin's first term was marked with consolidation of political power and stabilization of Russia's severely damaged economy. During Yeltsin's presidency, Russia was in a serious state of disarray. Governmental inefficiency and corruption reached a peak during a 1998 economic crisis. Russia's international prestige was questioned, but Putin managed to bring some stability to the country. While some Western circles criticize him for borderline autocratic governance, Russians overwhelmingly support Putin's presidency. In the 2004 presidential elections, more than two-thirds of voters supported Putin, who was easily reelected for a second term. Some critics of the current government have raised concerns that Putin could change the constitution in order to stay in power after his current term expires. This, however, seems unlikely. Meanwhile, Russia has regained its place as an important geopolitical factor. Its political influence is particularly significant in the turbulent Middle East region.

6

Russia's Economy

AGRICULTURE
Rural Russia under the Tsars

Agriculture under the tsars in the mid-1800s was exceedingly backward and very inefficient. A Russian farmer produced enough food for himself, his family, and two other people in a good year. An American farmer at that time produced enough food for himself, his family, and 10 other people. The freeing of serfs in 1861 failed to improve the quality of rural life or provide agriculture with a sound economic base. Three major obstacles stood in the way of achieving economic stability:

(1) the inadequate size of landholdings given to liberated peasants;

(2) the crushing burden of land payments; and

(3) the innovation-stifling institution of the village commune.

The average size of a new farmer's land holding (farm) was 36 acres (14.6 hectares) for the whole family. This land was given to a farmer for a fee. However, to ensure payment for the land, the village commune was made responsible to a farmer's loan. The system that evolved deprived most individual farmers of any incentive to improve the land. Taxes and redemption payments (payments to the tsar for the land received) kept the individual or family broke. Rural poverty led to horrendous famines and peasant unrest.

A series of agrarian reform laws were instituted in 1906. Land payments were abolished and land reform was decreed. Farmers were encouraged to consolidate their scattered strips of land and to create compact, privately owned farms. Government credits were provided to finance the purchase of state land and estate land. Within a short span of time, these reforms had a profound effect upon agriculture. Gross agricultural output rose by about one-third. On the eve of World War I, the peasants of imperial Russia were becoming private farmers similar to those in Western Europe and the United States. Still, the farmer's standard of living was extremely low, illiteracy and ill health were widespread, and the farmer's "land hunger" was not satisfied.

Lenin's Agricultural Policies

To gain support of rural dwellers, in November 1917, the urban-based Bolshevik government nationalized all land in Soviet Russia. The expropriated land was not given to the farmers. It remained in the hands of the state. Huge state farms and state-directed cooperative farms were created. From World War I until 1921, successful farmers were discriminated against. Their produce was frequently confiscated. The gains of the earlier reforms were wiped out. Many farmers were forced to rejoin village communes.

Bolshevik agricultural policies resulted in a horrible famine between 1918 and 1921. Faced with mass famine in the urban industrial areas of Soviet Russia, Lenin introduced his New Economic Policy in 1921. Under this policy, agriculture recovered from the damage done by "War Communism," in which the government had taken farm products without paying for them. By 1928, agricultural production had been restored to its 1913 level.

Collectivization under Stalin

The Communist Party needed capital to finance its plans to industrialize the Soviet Union. Many Bolsheviks favored paying for the new factories and mines by forcibly taking agricultural products from the peasants. After much debate within the party, the method chosen to finance industrial growth was Stalin's policy of all-out socialization of agriculture. An institutional "revolution from above" was initiated in the winter of 1929. The Stalin model required all farmers to become members of a state farm (government-operated specialty farm) or a collective farm (a farmer-operated, cooperative general farm). An official state policy allowed the taking of all land and other possessions belonging to the kulaks (prosperous private farmers). Many kulaks were deported.

In March 1929, 8 percent of rural households were collectivized. In January 1930, the figure was 21 percent. By March 1930, 58 percent had been collectivized. Force was widely used. Administrative decrees and tax discrimination against individual peasants resulted in an almost complete elimination of private farming. As a direct result of forced collectivization, a severe famine took place in 1933–1934, during which at least 9 million people died.

To make sure urban industrial workers had food and to assure state control of a stable food source, state farms were

By the mid-1930s, many farms in the Soviet Union had been converted to collectives, which were supervised by the government. Pictured here are women harvesting grain on a Soviet collective farm in 1936.

created on expropriated landed estates. Giant "grain factories," "meat factories," and "technical crop factories" were created. The state took absolute control of a sizable portion of the nation's agricultural output and marketing. These massive farm "factories" were to be completely mechanized and would serve as model farms. They employed paid rural workers (who held jobs similar to those in factories). The performance of these farm factories was highly unsatisfactory, however. Failing to serve the needs of the state, many state farms were converted into collective farms in the mid-1930s. They played a minor role in Soviet agriculture until the mid-1950s. By the late 1950s, a system of socialized agriculture evolved into the forms that existed within the Soviet Union until its collapse in 1991.

All farmland previously owned by peasants was cultivated in common, except for small private household plots of less than one acre (0.4 hectares) each. In 1956, these privately held plots accounted for less than 4 percent of the farmland within the Soviet Union. However, they produced 67 percent of the potato output, 55 percent of the milk, 57 percent of the meat, and 87 percent of the eggs. In most areas of the country, the only income earned by farm households from the early 1930s to the mid-1950s came from the sale of products from their private plots. Each farmer quickly learned to do only a minimum of the required, uncompensated work on a collective farm. Farmers concentrated most of their energies on very intensively cultivating their private plots, on which they also raised animals.

During World War II, Germans occupied most of the richest farmland in the Soviet Union. Farms were destroyed and fields were ruined. Agricultural output in 1945 was only 61 percent of the 1940 level.

Stalin strengthened the law of economic discrimination against rural dwellers. His actions led to the "Great Ukrainian Famine" of 1946–1947. This politically induced famine killed nearly 2 million Soviets.

Agricultural policies after World War II strengthened the government's control. Income was transferred from the rural to the urban sector. In 1952, agricultural production was only 0.7 percent above the 1940 level. During the same period, industrial production doubled. Barriers that limited productivity developed at all levels of the Soviet agricultural system. Nine million rural dwellers migrated to cities between 1950 and 1954. The population influx increased the demand for food in urban areas, while it also reduced the rural labor force available to produce the needed food.

Khrushchev's "Virgin Lands Project"

Stalin's death in 1953 led to a period in which the members of the Communist Party inner circle decided who would lead the Soviet Union. The man chosen was Nikita Khrushchev, who became the leader of both the Communist Party and the country. Khrushchev had a sincere desire to substantially improve the Soviet people's diet. In order to increase the availability of reasonably priced food, he ordered livestock production to be increased (for meat and milk). More vegetables and fruits were also to be grown. More animal feed crops were to be planted to support livestock and poultry production. Khrushchev directed that corn replace winter wheat crops in Ukraine. In fact, corn was to be planted anywhere it might grow. To replace the wheat lost to corn planting, Khrushchev initiated the "Virgin Lands Project" in the steppe and semidesert areas of Russia and northern Kazakhstan. This project involved plowing up never-tilled lands and planting spring wheat.

In this dry to semiarid vegetal zone, land could be plowed, planted, and harvested in one year. From 1954 to 1958, more than 100 million acres (40.5 million hectares) of new land were placed under cultivation. Yields were low per acre, but so many acres of land were sown that wheat production increased dramatically.

The diet of ordinary Soviets improved markedly. Khrushchev also introduced economic reforms that provided more machinery, fertilizers, and better seeds for agriculture. He gave farmers cash incentives to produce more. A series of favorable weather and political events helped bring success. In 1958, farmers harvested 50 percent more agricultural products than in 1953 just before Khrushchev assumed control of the Soviet government.

Brezhnev's "Nonblack Earth Program"

Khrushchev was removed from power and replaced by Leonid Brezhnev in 1964. Brezhnev had been secretary of the Central Committee of the Kazakhstan Communist Party during the initial years of the "Virgin Lands Project." When he came to power, he immediately raised the prices paid to farmers for their products and guaranteed a wage for collective farmers. His main goal was to revamp agriculture and rural life in the nonblack earth region of north European Russia. This cool, humid portion of the Soviet Union did not often experience drought. It had considerable potential for high agricultural production. Land reclamation on a large scale was necessary in this swampy, heavily glaciated area, however. To begin the process, drainage systems were laid, roads constructed, and new villages founded. High-quality seeds and fertilizers were made available to those who farmed here. Although a great deal of capital was invested, the returns turned out to be disappointing. This area has remained one of the poorest rural areas of Russia.

Gorbachev's "New Food Program"

Mikhail Gorbachev, who became the Soviet leader in 1985, had a strong background in agriculture. He had served as the Politburo's member in charge of agriculture before he became first secretary of the Communist Party. The Politburo was the highest governing body of the Communist Party. Gorbachev attempted to increase incentives for farmers to produce more food and to improve the Soviet diet. His "new food program" attempted to provide a diet that would compare with that of an American citizen. Gorbachev believed that inefficiency was the main problem of Soviet agriculture. He noted that 20 to 40 percent of all agricultural products were lost each year during harvesting, storage, or in transit to markets. To move perishable fruits and vegetables from the southern agricultural regions to the northern industrial cities, he ordered more refrigerated trucks and railroad cars to be manufactured. He had urban storage facilities constructed. He also directed that massive "greenhouse" complexes be built in the suburbs of Soviet cities to provide fresh vegetables during the winter months. Though he made many reforms, Gorbachev failed primarily because he retained the collective and state farm systems.

In 1985, Mikhail Gorbachev became leader of the Soviet Union. The recipient of the 1990 Nobel Peace Prize for instituting policies of openness (glasnost) and restructuring (perestroika), Gorbachev also created a "new food program" in which he increased incentives for farmers to produce more food.

Yeltsin's Plans to Privatize Agriculture in Russia

Boris Yeltsin, who led Russia after the fall of the Soviet Union, directed all state agencies involved to submit suggestions on how to reform Russian agriculture. This was part of his effort to privatize agriculture. His 1991 decree guaranteed Russian farmers the opportunity to become independent of the state agricultural system. This decree led to a decline in agricultural production and caused chaos in rural Russia. In January 1994, nearly 500,000 former state and collective farmworkers owned land. By the end of the 1994 agricultural year, at least 150,000 independent Russian farmers went bankrupt. The proposed model for breaking up collective farms rested upon three principles:

(1) Farmers must be free to choose how to reorganize the farm.

(2) Redistribution of land and assets must be open and honest.

(3) Outsiders must be excluded from the first stage of a farm breakup.

The transition to a free-market economy has generally hurt agriculture. Rural dwellers have suffered more than any other segment of the economy. The old system of socialized agriculture was irrational, but Yeltsin's new system exhibited a frustrating lack of a system. To make matters worse, Yeltsin entrusted agricultural reform to an administrator who later emerged as the leading opponent of change in the agricultural system. An even larger obstacle is the sheer complexity of turning 8 million people who depend on collective and state employment into private farmers. The agricultural crisis has resulted in regional and urban food shortages. Urban quality of life has declined because of the food shortages and the increased cost of food available.

Agriculture in Russia in the Early Twenty-First Century

Russia is a major importer of food. In most years, at least 20 percent of all food consumed is imported. Russia buys food from the United States, western European countries, and the former Soviet republics.

Agriculture in Russia faces severe climatic limitations. As a result, average productivity per acre is much lower in Russia than in the United States. Yearly agricultural production in

Russia varies greatly. Some years, production is three times more than average. Then, in other years, production drops to one-third of the average. The bulk of Russia's farm products are produced in areas climatically similar to the northern Great Plains of the United States (North Dakota and Montana). Russia produces much less food per acre and animal products per animal than does the United States. For most major crops, Russian yields are 50 to 80 percent lower per acre. Even the milk yield per cow is 40 to 50 percent lower than in the United States. As a result of these serious problems, Russian citizens face periodic food shortages.

Russia is a highly urbanized country that cannot adequately feed its people. Roughly 25 percent of Russia's people live in rural areas and 13 percent work on farms. In contrast, about 25 percent of U.S. residents live in rural areas, but fewer than 2 percent work on farms. In 2001, a Russian farmer produced enough food to feed six people. At the same time, an American farmer could feed more than 170 people. Russia's agricultural underperformance is tremendous, resulting in much rural poverty. The breakup of the Soviet Union left Russia with little productive agricultural land. Less than 8 percent of the nation's vast territory can be used for crop farming. The current problems in rural Russia will have a significant impact on the country's economic future. Considerable state investments in agriculture are needed to improve the food-producing capabilities of Russia's land.

Attempts have been made since 1991 to reform collective and state farms. When they were offered a number of options by the government, most collective and state farms opted to change their status. Many reorganized themselves as farm-worker partnerships, joint-stock farm companies, or farmer cooperatives. Not many private household farms were created.

In spite of changes in legal status, there has been little real change in the way farming is done. Russian farmers, in general, are unwilling or unable to take the risk of establishing private farms. Those who work to become independent producers like American farmers face hostility from their neighbors and local officials. Today, at least, private farming is not a practical option in rural Russia.

Agricultural production has disappointed Putin and other reformers in the Russian government. Bread is the basis of the Russian diet. Today, however, Russia must continue to import grain and other food for its people and feed for animals.

To improve their diets, many city dwellers have purchased small plots of land in the countryside to grow their own food. Urban food shortages and high food prices have encouraged those who live in cities to return to the land. This trend to an urban semisubsistence form of life reveals the seriousness of Russia's food-producing problem.

Russian government subsidies to agriculture remain huge, yet almost 50 percent of agricultural enterprises operated at a financial loss in 2000. This is an amazing percentage. With few exceptions, per-capita consumption of basic foodstuffs is lower today than in 1991. It will be decades before Russia can increase agricultural production to a point where it will raise living standards.

INDUSTRY AND INDUSTRIAL REGIONS
Industrial Historical Geography

Russia's Industrial Revolution began during the 1700s. Before this time, manufacturing was done at home by hand, using simple machines. Most pre–Industrial Revolution artisans and skilled laborers worked in rural areas. They made the products needed by their family, friends, and those who lived in their village. The use of complex, expensive, and large power-driven machines took manufacturing out of the home and brought it into factories or mills. Factories were designed to bring together raw materials, machines, and workers to produce a marketable product. The factory system enabled more things to be produced at less cost. In two centuries, the Industrial

Revolution changed Russia from a rural-agricultural society into an urban-industrial one. Russian workers were skilled and hardworking, but poorly paid. Products were sold at high prices. Profits were huge. Many early investors, bankers, and even noblemen became very rich. In the late 1800s and early 1900s, Russian factory owners were called "capitalists," or in some cases, "robber barons."

The first of the six phases in industrial development occurred during the reign of Peter the Great (1696–1725). Numerous ironworks and factories were established with the aid of western European technicians. The two major centers of metal production were the Urals and Tula-Moscow. Imperial Russia became the world's leading producer of iron. Copper was mined and smelted in the Urals. Metal fabricating works were set up in St. Petersburg, Moscow, and Nizhni Novgorod. Linen and woolen textile mills were established at Moscow, Yaroslavl, and Ivanovo. Glass, paper, and leather goods were manufactured in small factories throughout the empire. After Peter the Great's death, industrial growth and technical progress slowly fell behind that of western Europe and North America.

The second phase of industrial development began more than 100 years later. It lasted from 1860 until 1913. The American Civil War helped spark this period of rapid industrial expansion. Discovery of vast deposits of minerals and precious metals, combined with the world's need for foodstuffs, fueled the growth. Overall industrial production increased to 10 times its starting level. The most dramatic increases occurred between 1895 and 1913. Coal production increased by 100 times from 300,000 tons in 1861 to 29 million tons in 1913. Pig iron increased from 484,000 tons to 4.5 million tons. Steel production reached 4.6 million tons. In 1861, oil output was 30,000 tons. In 1913, it was 300 times larger, at 9 million tons.

At the dawn of the twentieth century, imperial Russia was the world's leading oil-producing nation. Moscow became one of the largest textile centers in the world. It produced nearly 30 percent of Russia's industrial goods. Tula and Lipetsk were the largest metal-fabricating centers. Riga became an engineering and shipbuilding center. The Eastern Ukraine Industrial Region was second only to the Moscow Region. By 1913, eastern Ukraine produced 70 percent of Russia's iron and fabricated more than half of its steel. Almost 90 percent of Russia's coal came from eastern Ukraine. By 1913, the Urals Industrial Region made only about 20 percent of the country's total iron and steel.

The third phase of industrial development began in 1928 with the first Five-Year Plan. It ended with the German invasion of the Soviet Union in 1941. World War I, the Russian Revolution of 1917, the civil war, and the impact of War Communism destroyed large sectors of the industrial base. As a result, during the mid-1920s, much debate took place over how the Soviet economy should be rebuilt and developed in the future. It became apparent that, to survive, the Soviet Union needed industrialization on a scale far beyond anything ever before achieved. The Communist Party decided to begin a rapid industrialization program that concentrated on heavy industry. The long-term interests of the Soviet state were considered more important than consumer needs. This governmental decision defined the Five-Year Plans from 1928 on. Little investment went toward consumer needs or agriculture. The first Five-Year Plan (1928–1932) strengthened preexisting industrial regions. The Five-Year Plans that followed expanded industrial production in the Ural Mountains and in the Kuzbass (Kuznetsk) region of western Siberia. Industrial growth during the 1930s was tremendous. By 1941, the Soviet Union was again one of the most powerful industrial nations in the world.

The fourth phase of industrial development was triggered by the German invasion of the Soviet Union in 1941. A wholesale evacuation of industrial plants was undertaken in 1941 and 1942. An estimated 1,360 major industrial plants were relocated: 455 were sent to the Urals, 200 to the Volga River Valley near Kazan, 210 to western Siberia around Omsk, and 250 to Kazakhstan and central Asia. These relocated plants and the plants constructed during the 1930s primarily handled war material production. The Urals Industrial Region and the Kuzbass Industrial Region provided 75 percent of the country's coal, iron, and steel toward the war effort. A number of significant industrial shifts took place at this time, notably the development of the Volga-Ural oil field. It replaced the German-threatened Caucasus and Baku oil fields. The invading German Army destroyed the industrial base of Ukraine, the Baltic states, Belarus, and western Russia. Industrial recovery after World War II was difficult. In 1946, total industrial production was only 75 percent of the 1940 level.

The fifth phase of industrial development began in 1946. It continued unevenly until the Soviet Union broke up in 1991. Stalin insisted on maintaining the focus on heavy industry laid out in the first three Five-Year Plans. After Stalin's death in 1953, Soviet planners slowly increased the growth of consumer goods industries. Khrushchev and Brezhnev continued rapid industrial development. Between 1954 and 1974, industrial output increased more than 700 percent. More than 60 percent of all industrial growth since 1917 actually took place during the 1960s. The 1970s and 1980s brought the Soviet Union to industrial maturity. The country progressed beyond coal, iron, and steel production. It developed new sources of energy, new raw materials, and new products. Continuous technological advances boosted the economy. In the 1980s, the Soviet Union was the world's second-most powerful industrial nation.

The sixth phase of industrial development began in 1991, and continues to evolve. Russia is the most industrialized of the former Soviet republics. Still, Russian industrial output declined sharply after 1991. The 1993 level of output was less than two-thirds the 1989 level. The decline in Russian industrial output was related to:

(1) fewer defense contracts and military hardware needs;

(2) disruption of trade related to the breakup of the Soviet Union;

(3) decrease in demand for manufactured consumer goods;

(4) huge price increases; and

(5) decline in Russian consumer income.

Russia's industrial base (factories and mills) is technically old and generally run-down. It must be modernized if the country hopes to compete in the international market.

In 2006, about one in five Russians was employed in industry (21 percent of total employment). Great internal struggles to transfer industry from a socialist, planned system to a capitalist free-market system continue to plague Russia.

In spite of all its problems, Russia remains one of the world's major industrial nations. Competing in a global economy, Russia manufactures products that include:

(1) a complete range of mining and extractive industry products such as coal, oil, gas, chemicals, and metals;

(2) machines that build machines (steel-rolling mills, high-performance aircraft, space vehicles, mills, and fabricators);

(3) shipbuilding;

(4) road and rail transportation equipment;

(5) communications equipment;

(6) agricultural equipment such as tractors, combines, and implements;

(7) construction equipment such as special trucks, earth-moving equipment, and road-paving equipment;

(8) electrical power generating and transmitting equipment (atomic electrical plants, dynamos, and pylons);

(9) medical and scientific instruments;

(10) consumer durables such as radios, television sets, refrigerators, and stoves;

(11) textiles;

(12) foodstuffs; and

(13) handicrafts.

Russia is a vast country with a great wealth of mineral resources. It has a well-educated workforce, a diverse industrial base, and eventually, it will make the transition to a modern world market economy.

Russian Industrial Regions

The present pattern of industrial location in Russia was set during the early Five-Year Plans. Distinct industrial regions remain, based on their industrial history. They are

(1) old centers of market-oriented, labor-intensive industries;

(2) old centers of heavy industry;

(3) new energy-based industrial regions; and

(4) emerging industrial regions.

These regions represent a decision-making struggle. Industrial planners wanted to locate new plants at the most logical sites. Politicians, on the other hand, wanted to spread industry as widely as possible throughout the Soviet Union, in the hope that all ethnic groups would benefit from industrial progress.

Old Centers of Market-Oriented, Labor-Intensive Regions

Moscow (the Central Industrial Region) is the most important "old center of market-oriented, labor-intensive industries." Despite having few natural resources, Moscow developed industrially before the 1917 revolution. A central location and its function as capital of the Soviet Union stimulated modern industrial growth and expansion. In 1991, the region accounted for approximately 20 percent of Soviet industrial output. Moscow is an engineering, textile, manufacturing, and communications center. In 2000, the Central Industrial Region produced 35 percent of Russia's total industrial output.

St. Petersburg (the Northwestern Industrial Region) is the second "old center of market-oriented, labor-intensive industries." Peter the Great built the city and its initial industries. As the capital of imperial Russia, it benefited from Peter's desire to quickly modernize Russia. With few natural resources, St. Petersburg developed labor-intensive industries. The city also became a shipbuilding center. There were highly technical engineering and fabricating plants. It became a center of high-quality machine manufacturing. Research and development flourished. By 1991, St. Petersburg was producing approximately 5 percent of all Soviet industrial goods. In 2000, the St. Petersburg region produced 10 percent of Russia's total industrial output.

Old Centers of Heavy Industry

Unlike Moscow and St. Petersburg, the "old centers of heavy industry" have rich resources of coal, iron ore, and other minerals. Historically, the most famous is the Urals Industrial Region. It lies astride the 1,500-mile-long (2,414-kilometer-long) Ural Mountains. After Moscow, the Urals Industrial Region is the second-most important in Russia. This region produces a wide spectrum of minerals. It is Russia's primary source of iron and steel. It has many different manufacturing industries. In 1991, the Urals region was responsible for about 4 percent of total Soviet industrial production. Intensive industrial use has nearly exhausted the region's coal, iron ore, and critical minerals. Nevertheless, a large industrial base helps this region retain its position as a leading producer of iron, steel, and heavy industrial goods. In 2000, the Urals Industrial Region produced more than 15 percent of Russia's total industrial output.

New Energy-Based Industrial Regions

World War II industrial relocation created the "new energy-based industrial regions." These regions were situated beyond the reach of invading German troops. They include the dispersed Kuzbass and Surgut Industrial Region and the Yenisey-Baikal (Eastern Siberian) Industrial Region. Oil and gas fields that extend from Surgut to Urengoy supply much of western Europe's natural gas. The Kuznetsk coalfields and the Tom River Valley iron ore deposits of western Siberia abound in mineral resources. Together, these regions made up nearly 8 percent of total industrial production in 1991. The Eastern Siberian Industrial Region contributed 10 percent of Russia's industrial output in 2000. It also supplied more than half of the nation's gas, oil, and coal.

The Yenisey-Baikal (Eastern Siberian) Industrial Region was not important before World War II. The postwar emphasis on oil, natural gas, and electric power speeded its development. This region has the greatest hydroelectric power potential in Russia. Abundant cheap energy attracted chemical and nonferrous metallurgy industries to the region. The area also possesses enormous reserves of nonferrous metal ores. These include gold, platinum, silver, nickel, and copper. In 1991, the region accounted for 7 percent of overall industrial output. By 2000, that figure dropped to 5 percent.

Emerging Industrial Regions

The end of the cold war has created "emerging industrial regions." The need for internal manufactured goods is changing. There are new economic opportunities. One new area is the North Caucasus Industrial Region, which is focused upon the territory of Krasnodar and Novorossiysk. It is becoming a significant center for the production and transmission (by means of pipelines) of oil and gas. The region produced about 12 percent of Russia's industrial output in 2000. It produces chemicals, food processing, petrochemicals, iron ore, and machinery.

The Vladivostok (Far East) Industrial Region has not yet developed to its full potential. In 1991, it accounted for 5 percent of Soviet industrial output. Its industrial development has focused upon the markets in Japan, Korea, and China. Investors support low-volume, high-value products, such as gold, diamonds, tin, and mercury. Vast quantities of wood and wood products are also exported, as well as fish and crab. In 2000, the Far East Economic Region accounted for more than 4 percent of Russia's industrial output.

MINERAL RESOURCES

Russia is extremely well endowed in mineral resources. It is rich in coal and oil, and in most raw materials required by a modern industrial nation. A determined effort was made in the 1930s to survey and map mineral wealth. Vast deposits of coal, oil, and natural gas were discovered. Soviet geologists reported that the nation contained more than one-half of the world's total reserves of coal and lignite. They also reported that the Soviet Union contained two-fifths of the world's crude petroleum and natural gas reserves. Under Stalin and

The Kuzbass region, located in the Kemerovo Oblast Province of western Siberia, is responsible for the production of approximately 40 percent of Russia's coal, or nearly 44 tons annually. Pictured here is the Yesaulskaya mine, near the town of Novokuznetsk, which is about 1,850 miles (3,000 kilometers) west of Moscow.

Khrushchev, coal was the single most important energy source in the Soviet Union. Of the surveyed coal reserves, 65 percent were either anthracite (a hard coal) or bituminous (a softer coking coal). The remaining 35 percent of coal reserves were subbituminous coal and lignite. Coal deposits were not found in all regions of the country. More than 90 percent was in

Russia, east of the Ural Mountains. During the first Five-Year Plan, the Kuzbass (or Kuznetsk Basin, southeast of Novosibirsk) was put into production. This unique basin had huge deposits of high-grade coal in very thick and accessible coal seams. Soviet geologists also reported that the Tunguska Basin and the Lena Basin, both in north-central Siberia, contained the world's largest untapped coalfields.

Recognizing the significance of the Soviet Union's vast reserves of oil and natural gas, Soviet planners decided that coal should no longer be the nation's most important energy source. In the late 1960s, 1970s, and 1980s, development focused on new oil and natural gas fields and on pipelines. In the 1980s, Soviet geologists reported that the Soviet Union contained 25 percent of the world's oil reserves. From tsarist times until the late 1940s, the Baku Field on the western shore of the Caspian Sea was the leading oil field. In the late 1950s, the Volga-Ural Field in Russia became the Soviet Union's largest producer. In the 1980s, the West Siberian Field became the leading source of Soviet oil. Oil had been discovered in the West Siberian Field (Tyumen-Surgut area) in the late 1950s. Commercial production began in the mid-1960s. Development of this vast oil field in the 1980s was one of the most spectacular achievements of Soviet industry after World War II. Oil reserves in the Lena Field are limited. The Lena area is also very remote. There are large offshore deposits in the Arctic region beneath the Sea of Okhotsk (primarily between Sakhalin Island and the Kamchatka Peninsula). Increased oil and natural gas production led to a rapid expansion of the Soviet Union's petrochemical industry. In 1991, the Soviet Union was the world's largest coal and oil producer.

Russia, in the early years of the twenty-first century, is self-sufficient in energy and is a leading world producer of energy fuels. Russian oil and natural gas output equaled about 20 percent of the world's total in the 1990s. Today, Russia exports more than 35 percent of all oil and natural gas extracted. In contrast, the United States imports nearly 25 percent of the energy it needs. The United States produces about 30 percent less oil than Russia and 20 percent less natural gas.

Energy, primarily oil and natural gas, represents Russia's largest source of revenue. As the second-largest exporter of oil, after Saudi Arabia, Russia has managed to fill its coffer with hard currency in recent years. In 2004, for example, oil companies produced 9.27 million barrels per day, of which 6.67 million barrels were exported. Unexpectedly high oil and natural gas prices contributed to a vast budget surplus allowing the government to create an account that has grown to billions of dollars. This money, called a stabilization fund, is used to repay foreign debt, which is still more than 100 billion in U.S. dollars, and for various reconstruction projects. By the end of 2006, it is expected to reach $75 billion. Financial benefits from high energy prices have helped the country to establish the world's fourth-largest gold and foreign currency reserves.

Serious issues exist, however, in regard to the energy sector. First, Russia's economy is overwhelmingly dependent upon oil and natural gas revenues. Were a major decrease in production to occur, or if energy prices dropped sharply, the whole economy could suffer serious damage. Second, most of the energy infrastructure suffered from years of inadequate maintenance and requires modernization. Finally, and seemingly paradoxical, the stabilization fund must be carefully, and slowly, distributed or otherwise Russia may experience yet another economic crisis. One would imagine that more money spent means that life will be better for Russians, but the economic reality is often much different. If the government opens the fund in order to promote public projects (such as infrastructure and transportation) and does that rapidly, sudden inflation will be triggered. Such conditions ultimately would lead to economic destabilization and a further decrease in the quality of life of ordinary Russians.

Mineral resources vary greatly from one region to another within Russia. Iron ore is widely distributed. The most important deposits are in the Ural Mountains, within the Kuzbass (Kuznetsk Basin) of southwestern Siberia, and at Tula (south of Moscow). Russia has the largest iron ore reserves in the world. Chrome ore, used in the manufacture of metals, is mined in the Ural Mountains. Nickel comes from the town of Nikel in the Kola Peninsula (south of Murmansk), from the southern Ural Mountains, and from Norilsk (at the mouth of the Yenisey River in Siberia). Russia ranks second in the world in the production of nickel. Nonferrous other metals are also plentiful. Copper is mined at numerous sites in the Ural Mountains and in eastern Siberia. Significant deposits of bauxite (aluminum) are found in the Kola Peninsula, southwest of St. Petersburg, and in the northern Ural Mountains. Gold and magnesium are mined in Siberia and the Far East. Russia was once the world's second-largest producer of gold but now is the fifth largest. The location of resources and their climates hinder Russia from increasing the production of oil, natural gas, and minerals. Most of Russia's fuel reserves and mineral reserves are located in Siberia and the Far East. These regions have cold, harsh climates. They are also far from major market centers.

TRANSPORTATION
Inland Waterways

The Kievan state, Moscow, and Novgorod all became rich and politically powerful because of river trade. Every major city in imperial Russia and in the Soviet Union was initially located on a river or another major body of water. The Volga River system opened the way to the riches of the Middle East, central Asia, and China. It also led to the Urals, to Siberian furs, and to Imperial Russia's first major ironworks. St. Petersburg was founded as a port city. The tsarist government devoted centuries to creating man-made water links between the Black Sea, Caspian Sea, Baltic Sea, and White Sea. Until about a century ago, the great bulk of commercial traffic moved by rivers. Unfortunately, some Russian rivers are frozen over for at least six months of the year. Spring flooding and low water levels in late summer or early fall also reduce transportation efficiency. It is likely that future economic development will include further expansion of waterway transportation. This is the cheapest means of transportation, which is especially significant for a country of this enormous size. Sooner rather than later, one may assume, the vast areas east of the Ural Mountains will experience population growth, because of their immeasurable economic potential. When market forces collide and Siberia becomes economically attractive, people will begin to move into this now-remote region.

Road System

Muscovite princes recognized that a reliable, all-weather transportation network was crucial for political control and economic development. Although the distances involved were immense, there were few physical impediments to overland transportation routes in the west. On the other hand, climate, permafrost, and relief combined to present major obstacles in Siberia. Initially, roads were constructed to bring goods and products to river ports and to maintain military control. Alternating frost, snow, thaws, mud, and dust hindered road development. Road construction materials were scarce in places. Geology, weather, and climate, along with low population density, slowed construction of a functioning road system before the Russian Revolution. Overland transportation was busy only in winter when the ground was frozen or the snow compact. In 1917, the road system covered a distance of less than 18,000 miles (28,968 kilometers). During World War I, the Revolution, Civil War, and War Communism, the road system deteriorated. In 1928, the Soviet Union had 20,000 miles (32,187 kilometers) of gravel roads and only 6,000 miles (9,656 kilometers) of improved or paved roads.

Between 1928 and 1932, nearly 60,000 miles (96,560 kilometers) of roads were constructed, but road building in the 1930s was inadequate. World War II demonstrated the vital need for a good road system. This led Khrushchev and Brezhnev to make road building a high priority. By the mid-1960s, the Soviet road network had expanded to 220,000 miles (354,056 kilometers), but further expansion came slowly. Today, the country (which is about twice the size of the United States) has only about one mile of road for every six miles in the United States.

Russia's nearly 500,000-mile (804,672-kilometer) road system is terribly inadequate for a country of its size. The contemporary network requires improvements in existing roads and further expansion. There is a need for multilane highways and expressways to connect regional centers. Good roads are a key to successful development of remote areas. When built, they will increase individual mobility of Russia's population. The Soviet Union could not and sometimes did not want to pay to build new roads. Geographic mobility of population was not encouraged during the Soviet era. Russians tend to be much more stationary than Americans, who are extremely mobile. During the twentieth century, American society and family life revolved around the automobile, while automakers were the largest employers. In Russia and other Soviet republics, that was not the case. Instead of being an integral part of life, automobiles were generally considered a luxury few could own. The situation, however, is rapidly changing. Russia adopted capitalism in the 1990s and cars flooded into the country. New millionaires and billionaires are buying the world's most expensive vehicles. Mercedes sells more of its highest-priced models in Russia than in any other country. Ordinary people are purchasing less-expensive models, from local or international makers. Foreign automakers are eager to compete in the increasingly lucrative Russian market. In the spring of 2006, two heavyweights, General Motors and Volkswagen, announced the opening of plants in Russia. These projects are measured in hundreds of millions of dollars and will create thousands of new jobs. These companies join Ford and a number of European and

Asian makers already present in the Russian market. Development of the auto industry will stimulate highway projects and toll roads in which foreign investors will gladly participate, because such projects are large profit makers. Capitalism is providing a huge boost in (literally) connecting Russians.

Railroad System

Development of modern imperial Russia and of the Soviet Union depended almost entirely upon its railroad system. In a modern industrial society, where great distances separate resources from markets, transportation is extremely important. Compared with the problems faced in road construction and in river transportation, railroad construction problems were relatively slight. There were shortages of ballast stone for track beds and trees for railroad ties on the steppes. Still, these problems, as well as moving sands in central Asia and permafrost in Siberia, failed to hinder the development of an integrated railroad system. The first public railroad was constructed in 1837. It ran from St. Petersburg to the Imperial Palace (14 miles; 23 kilometers). Major railroad lines followed. They connected St. Petersburg to Moscow in 1851 and to Warsaw in 1861. Lines connected Moscow to Saratov in 1870, to Warsaw in 1871, and to the Crimea in 1875. By 1892, western imperial Russia enjoyed a functioning network of interconnected railroad lines. The tsar next decided that Siberia should be connected to Moscow. Construction of the Trans-Siberian Railroad began in 1892. By 1899, the railroad had reached Lake Baikal in southern Siberia. An all-Russian route to Vladivostok was not completed until 1916, but more railroad lines were constructed during the first Five-Year Plan. By 1939, the Trans-Siberian and many other existing lines had double tracks.

After World War II, railroad equipment improved considerably. Diesel and electric railroad engines were added. Major railroad routes were electrified. In 1960, railroads hauled more than 75 percent of Soviet freight. Almost 75 percent of passenger service was by rail. Despite the dominant role of railroads in the Soviet economic system, the rail network was not dense. Areas were unequally served. Very little railroad construction has taken place since the completion of the Baikal-Amur Mainline (BAM) in 1984.

Railroads are critical to Russia's current struggle for economic recovery. No other modern nation depends as heavily upon railroads to move goods and people as does Russia. Distances from production centers to consumers are enormous. Distances from mineral deposits and energy fields to international markets are equally large. The Russian rail system needs a complete upgrading, but many problems continue to reduce the efficiency of railroad transportation. However, understanding the strategic importance of the country's network, the national railway companies recently began an ambitious program of reconstruction. Foreign investors are willing to invest in modernization of established routes, Moscow to St. Petersburg in particular. Various Western companies are also in the process of financing the creation of new routes for transportation of people and goods. In 2005, the European Bank for Reconstruction and Development brought additional credibility to the future of Russian railways by providing millions of dollars in investments. By 2020, Russia is expected to have a well-developed network of modern railroads. Much of the development will be in European parts of the country, but there also will be links to China and its booming economy.

Air Transportation System

Air transportation played an important role in uniting the far-flung and remote areas of the Soviet Union. It began to develop prior to the Russian Revolution. Growth continued during the years between World Wars I and II and it expanded greatly after World War II. In the 1970s, the Soviet Union claimed to have more scheduled airline service than any other country in the world. In 1991, Moscow had direct air links to every large city

Once the world's largest airline carrier, Aeroflot overcame a number of problems in the 1990s, including poor service, and today serves more than 50 foreign countries. In addition, it is the only Russian airline to be a member of an international airline alliance—SkyTeam.

in the Soviet Union. Aeroflot, the official Soviet airline, was state-owned. It held world records for number of aircraft, distance flown, and passengers carried. Even so, air transportation accounted for only a small percentage of the total goods transported in the Soviet Union. The breakup of the Soviet Union disrupted the integrated all-union air system. Every former Soviet republic has now formed its own airline, or linked with other republics to form new airlines. After years of mismanagement, Aeroflot (today, Russia's official airline) is finally emerging as a sound carrier. It has upgraded its aircraft, purchasing U.S. and western European planes. Aeroflot has succeeded in recovering from a very difficult, disruptive period in the early 1990s.

Russia benefits tremendously from its air transportation system. It would be unable to operate on a day-to-day basis without a well-developed network. Roads and railroads are important, but because of the vast distances to be covered, air transportation is the backbone of Russia's network for carrying both people and goods. Eleven time zones are quickly spanned by plane, but it takes a full week to travel from Moscow to Vladivostok by railroad. Some cities in northeastern Russia will never have any connection except air links to the outside world. They are too remote and have too few people to economically justify building and maintaining modern ground connections.

Merchant Marine Transport System

The spread of Communism and economic growth within the Soviet Union after World War II led to a large expansion of foreign trade. Turnover of goods at Soviet seaports increased five times between 1960 and 1975. Development of Siberian and Far Eastern resources also stimulated additional movement of goods on coastal shipping routes and between ports on different seas. The Northern Sea Route was very important to Soviet planners. It linked together ports located on the northern coast of western Russia and Siberia. Unfortunately, this sea route is open only three months a year. Icebreakers are required to maintain shipping channels. In 1991, there were 66 seaports in the Soviet Union. However, only 28 ports handled 96 percent of the foreign trade. Oil, timber and raw materials, military hardware, and machinery were the major products shipped from Soviet ports in 1991. Most ports have been equipped to handle container ships.

Russia has few seaports that can handle international shipping year-round. Murmansk, north of the Arctic Circle in northwestern Russia, is ice-free, but is located far from the internal Russian markets. St. Petersburg is Russia's most important seaport. However, its harbor freezes over with very thick ice for months during the winter. Kaliningrad, located between Poland and Lithuania, is a relatively ice-free port, but, like Murmansk, it is isolated. Novorossiysk, on the Black Sea, is ice-free, but far from Moscow. Vladivostok, located on the Sea of Japan, has a perfect natural harbor. However, it is not close to the population center of Russia. Russia has always been in need of a good warm-water seaport. The lack of such access to the major markets of the world continues to hinder Russia's socioeconomic development.

7

Reconstructing Socioeconomic Unity

ATTEMPTS TO ORGANIZE THE RUSSIAN CULTURAL REALM

The Soviet Union was the successor to the sprawling imperial Russian Empire. Guided by Marxist ideology and the Communist Party, Soviet leaders attempted to remold the economy, cultural life, and settlement. Centralized national planning was their major tool.

Soviet planners recognized the problems caused by Russia's size. During the Five-Year Plans, they constructed roads, canals, railroads, and air routes, and built thousands of new urban centers. They remolded rural life by socializing agriculture. However, internal discontent with Communist rule, ethnic groups with dreams of independence, and the realization that the Soviet system was too rigid to follow modern economic trends led to the disintegration of the Soviet Union. Soviet leaders failed to overcome the problems associated with the nation's size, ethnic diversity, and unlinked places. Today, Russian Federation leaders must not repeat those same mistakes.

More than 10 years after the breakup of the Soviet Union, Russian Federation leaders have developed a number of plans they hope will restore socioeconomic unity and increase prosperity. These plans include:

(1) strengthening the Commonwealth of Independent States (CIS);

(2) creating an East European Common Market (EECM);

(3) intensifying Russian Federation socioeconomic and political integration; and

(4) forging a geopolitical and economic partnership with the United States.

THE COMMONWEALTH OF INDEPENDENT STATES (CIS)

The Commonwealth of Independent States (CIS) succeeded the Soviet Union. It was founded by Russia, Ukraine, and Belarus in December 1991. The CIS has a population of 280 million and an area of 8.5 million square miles (13.7 million square kilometers). All former Soviet republics except Lithuania, Latvia, and Estonia joined the organization. The Baltic republics elected to tie their future to integration with other European groups, primarily the European Union and NATO. President Vladimir Putin has stated that expanding ties with the other CIS nations remains Russia's absolute priority. This makes sense, because the city of Moscow is the natural nucleus for the integration of former Soviet republics.

The Commonwealth of Independent States is an international organization made up of 12 former Soviet Republics—Armenia, Azerbaijan, Belarus, Georgia, Kazakhstan, Kyrgyzstan, Moldova, Russia, Tajikistan, Turkmenistan, Ukraine, and Uzbekistan—that was created after the dissolution of the Soviet Union in 1991. Pictured here are CIS leaders at a meeting in Moscow in July 2006. From left to right: President Vladimir Putin (Russia), President Emomali Rakhmonov (Tajikistan), President Vladimir Voronin (Moldova), President Alexander Lukashenko (Belarus), and President Ilham Aliev (Azerbaijan).

Improving the standard of living within the 12 former Soviet republics will happen only if they can overcome the legacy of 70 years of state domination of most aspects of life. Poorly managed industrial enterprises and agricultural units still hinder economic vitality. Many new countries within the CIS also have tumultuous political situations to overcome. The old-style party-state organization has slowed down progress and hindered change. Reforming each republic's economy is an absolute necessity for future growth. Because of the way the

Soviet Union's economy was organized, CIS members will continue to depend on the Russian Federation. They need its energy, raw materials, and financial aid.

Russia's relationship with its neighbors often generates political problems. With its size and power, it has the ability to influence CIS partners' internal affairs. Russia considers itself the main regional power and acts accordingly. Some former republics still host the Russian military, while others depend on Russia for their oil and natural gas distribution. In the winter of 2005, Russia suddenly increased the prices of energy exported to Ukraine, a move analysts labeled strictly political. Moscow justified its actions as simply being an attempt to create real market conditions for the export of its energy. Although the West criticized Russia for this action, the problem really stemmed from Ukraine's dependence upon Russian energy imports. Similarly, the European Union lacks sufficient energy production to meet its growing demands, a fact Russia manipulates for its own political and economic gains.

Despite political obstacles, the economic reality dictates a close relationship among CIS countries. They depend on Russia for the import of energy, but also for exports of their own products, because Russia is their biggest trade partner. This is particularly significant in central Asia and the Caucasus. The landlocked nature of those countries, and global competition, currently prevents their economic expansion beyond the Russian economic realm of more than 140 million consumers. In the aftermath of changes that led to the Soviet Union's dissolution, former republics expressed serious concern about the possibility of Russian military intervention throughout the region. As a remnant of the old Soviet structure, Russia had military bases in each of the newly independent countries. This fear, however, was unjustified. Russia kept removing troops and clearing out bases. Today, only small military facilities, the result of bilateral agreements, are present in some of the former republics.

Kazakhstan, because of the large presence of ethnic Russians, was perhaps the Soviet republic most concerned over its future when independence came in 1991. Now, however, the country holds an important strategic partnership with Russia. Its oil and natural gas are transported through Russian territory to Europe and elsewhere. Gazprom, the world's largest natural gas company, holds significant stakes in Kazakhstan's extraction and transport of fossil fuels. Moreover, the two countries are working closely to establish other mutually beneficial economic and political ties. Russia leases the land for its space station in Baikonur. Two countries agreed in 2006 to expand the joint space program. Presidents Vladimir Putin and Nursultan Nazarbayev acknowledged that the two countries will develop a commercial satellite launching system. Such a system will allow low-cost launching of smaller satellites directly from planes into space.

Russia and its neighbors have developed a mutual understanding that having a powerful neighbor next door helps everyone. It was Russia that limited the possibility for conflicts between former republics in the years of territorial consolidations. Although many internal conflicts existed, external conflicts remained limited. One can attribute the absence of such conflicts to Russia and its regional influence as a mediator.

RUSSIAN FEDERATION INTEGRATION

Some disorder and conflict has occurred within the Russian Federation. Many ethnic groups want independence from Russia. If that is not possible, they at least want more recognition and autonomy. Consolidation of power in the hands of Vladimir Putin nevertheless prevented major conflicts (other than the seemingly continuous unrest in the Caucasus region). During Boris Yeltsin's regime, many remote regions existed in semi-independence. The federal government's decisions were largely ignored. Although the process of stabilization is slowly occurring, few expect Moscow to lose its political grip.

Located in the far southwestern part of Russia, Chechnya is a republic
that declared independence from the Soviet Union when it collapsed in
1991. However, the Russian government has not recognized Chechnya's
sovereign status and the two sides have been fighting on and off since
the mid-1990s. Pictured here are Russian soldiers patrolling the Chechen
capital of Grozny in an armored personnel carrier in October 2005.

The most difficult internal issue continues to be the conflict in Chechnya, which has been occurring on and off since
the mid-1990s. Separatist movement in this southern republic
still creates a serious danger despite the presence of thousands
of heavily armed federal military and police forces. The Caucasus region never fully accepted its status after Russia occupied
the area during the nineteenth century as a part of its imperi-
alistic ambitions. The ethnic mosaic here is, perhaps, the most
complex in the world. It represents a powder keg that is ready
to explode at any time.

In terms of political integration, another issue that keeps
recurring is that of unification between Russia and Belarus.

Ever since the Soviet Union was dissolved in 1991 and the two former republics became independent, many have called for reunification. Although a majority of people on both sides would support referendums for unification, some significant issues still remain unresolved. The Russian government, for example, insists on Belarus's complete integration into the Russian state. Belarus's leadership, on the other hand, supports equal representation in the future political union.

Some problems regarding Russia's boundaries still exist. One of them is the issue of territory of the South Kuril Islands that the Soviet Union annexed in 1945. During the last days of World War II, Soviet forces occupied these islands that the Japanese considered to be theirs. To Russia, the claim represents the return of its territory lost in the war of 1904–05. Japan sees it as an issue that must be solved by returning to pre-1945 boundaries. In geopolitical terms, Russia benefits from controlling the islands, because they provide an adequate maritime corridor for the Russian Far East Fleet.

On the other hand, Russia's westernmost territory also creates problems. Once in the hands of Germans, Kaliningrad Oblast is an exclave, a part of Russia that is separated from the rest of the country by Lithuania and Belarus. Geographic isolation has contributed to serious economic and political handicaps. While other countries are joining the European Union, this part of Russia exists in isolation from both Europe and the rest of Russia.

GEOPOLITICAL AND GLOBAL ECONOMIC PARTNERSHIPS

Starting in the late 1940s, the United States and the Soviet Union clashed in political and economic conflict during the cold war. When the cold war ended, the Soviet Union disbanded. The United States gave token support to the Russian Federation. For 10 or so years, however, the United States paid little attention to Russia's socioeconomic problems.

On September 11, 2001, international terrorists struck New York City and Washington, D.C. Several thousand Americans and people from many other countries died. President George W. Bush directed the U.S. military to eliminate terrorist centers and bases in Afghanistan. When U.S. armed forces began to bomb Afghanistan, they entered Russia's realm of influence. President Bush and President Putin forged an alliance against international terrorists. At the same time, they also looked for opportunities to work together for global security. Russia welcomed American intervention in Afghanistan. It helped stabilize a turbulent part of the world viewed in Moscow as an immense danger for its interests in central Asia and neighboring regions. After the United States invaded Iraq in 2003, however, the Russian response was much cooler, because Moscow and Baghdad had a well-developed relationship lasting since Soviet times.

The dependence of the United States upon Middle East oil poses an economic threat to the American way of life. If there were a decrease in oil from the Middle East, the U.S. economy would suffer. President Bush recognized that Russia has vast oil and natural gas reserves, so he began to explore ways that the United States could finance oil and natural gas production in the CIS. President Putin saw that Russia, the CIS, and the United States would all reap benefits if they teamed up on selected political and economic activities. Since 2005, however, Russia's relationship with the United States has cooled. One of the major disagreements between the countries relates to Iran's nuclear program. While the American side portrays Iran as a foe and a supporter of terrorists, Russia has been developing stronger economic ties with this important Middle Eastern country.

Among the major initiatives during Putin's presidency is the restoration of Russia as a major world power, a position that plummeted during the years of Yeltsin's rule. The current administration has successfully reversed the downward trend.

Economic and political connections with North African and Middle Eastern countries have been revived. Russia and China are developing stronger ties on several fronts. As one of the largest importers of its military technology, China is concerned about friendship with Russia. In 2005, the two countries held joint large-scale military exercises, something previously unimaginable.

8

Russia
Looks Ahead

RUSSIA'S POTENTIAL

At the end of World War I, distinguished British geographer Sir Halford Mackinder published a volume entitled *Democratic Ideals and Reality*. In it, he proposed a "Heartland Theory." He contended that the country that controlled the "world island" (Eurasian continent) could control the world. He stated: "Who rules eastern Europe commands the Heartland. Who rules the Heartland commands the World Island. Who rules the World Island commands the world." Mackinder's Heartland includes all of Russia, most of the CIS, portions of Mongolia and north China, and the Middle East. This area is large and well supplied with raw materials. However, the population of the Heartland, according to Mackinder, would never be numerous in comparison to the other regions of the world.

Just as Mackinder's theory implied, Russia has great potential as a country. The CIS is also an excellent framework for economic linkage

After the September 11, 2001, terrorist attacks, the United States looked to Russia as a viable democratic-capitalist Asian ally. Pictured here are U.S. president George W. Bush and Russian president Vladimir Putin during a meeting at the White House two months after the attacks.

and market accessibility. In today's world, anything beyond a subsistence life requires trade and communications. As a result, the future of the Russian Federation and the CIS will be determined by geopolitics, geoeconomics, and the Russian Federation's internal reforms.

As part of those reforms, the Russian government has begun to create the means to secure funds to meet the nation's budget needs. Issues of national survival and political stability have forced government leaders to make hard decisions. New laws have been passed and a national educational campaign to increase state revenues is having some success. Even so, the greatest changes in Russia and the most significant improvements in the nation's self-respect have been the results of geopolitics and geoeconomics.

Politically marginalized for a decade, Russia regained international importance after the terrorist attacks of September 11, 2001. President Bush's decision to oust the government in Afghanistan that supported international terrorism changed American attitudes toward Russia. The United States needed a viable, supportive, democratic, capitalist ally in Asia. Russia was the logical choice, for reasons that included aspects of Mackinder's Heartland Theory. Location is the prime issue in geography. The physical position of a country at a time of international crisis is important in political policy and in economic orientation. Lord George Curzon, a British statesman, remarked that, in World War I, the Allies "floated to victory on a sea of oil." George Cressey, a noted regional geographer, stated that the Allies "flew to victory on a cloud of gasoline" in World War II. The economies of the United States and western Europe are based heavily upon oil and natural gas, which are inexpensive energy sources. The Russian Federation and the nations of the central Asian and Caucasus regions are exceptionally rich in these resources. Vast coalfields and large deposits of oil and natural gas lay waiting to be developed here. Russia and the CIS also have another great asset—their people—whose qualities are more important than their numbers. Those who live in Russia are well educated, literate, hardworking, and very patriotic. They excel in recognizing the assets and the liabilities of the Heartland area.

Russia's future geography will be determined in part by international politics and in part by international economics. Even more, however, the future will be decided by the peoples of Russia. Democracy, benevolent capitalism, personal freedoms, and prosperity must yet be fully earned, but the prospects for the Russian Federation are good. After so many years of economic hardship, ordinary Russians hope to begin seeing the proverbial "light at the end of the tunnel." Although many still live in poverty, especially in the countryside, Russia's peoples can expect an increase in their quality of life. On the bumpy road to prosperity, some major obstacles must be overcome.

Among the problems is Russian xenophobia, or fear of strangers. This is understandable considering the number of times Russia has been attacked from every direction. Mongols came from the east, French and Germans from the west, Turks from the south, just to name a few. The fear of strangers is deeply entrenched among most ethnic Russians and it affects the way society in general operates. This cultural behavior is counterproductive in the age of globalization when worldwide cultural boundaries are being eliminated. Complicated regulations limit travel to, from, and within the country and foreign workers are discouraged. Laws create barriers against international companies that are willing to invest in Russia's future. Many Russians believe that the process of globalization leads to loss of sovereignty, rather than providing benefits to the people. We can conclude, nevertheless, that incoming generations of young Russians will overcome the burden of the past. They will not remember the cold war and other turbulent times. Instead, their popular-culture-oriented lifestyle will make them citizens of the world, therefore fundamentally changing Russian culture.

This trend is already obvious in large urban areas such as Moscow and St. Petersburg. These cities are directly impacted by global changes. The countryside, on the other hand, will require more time to experience a cultural transformation and become integrated into the modernization process. Country folk everywhere tend to be suspicious of changes that may affect the existing way of life, especially demographic changes such as an increase in immigrant populations. Rural Russians are not an exception. Elsewhere in this book, Russia's demographic problem of declining numbers has been spotlighted. Somehow, this issue must be addressed. Without an adequate number of people to enter the labor force, the country faces a

With the cold war but a distant memory, Russia will look to the future and move toward becoming part of the global community. Young people, such as those who work for St. Petersburg's Angels tourist service, will continue to offer a helping hand to Russia's many visitors.

huge economic challenge. At a time when many economic indicators are showing rapid increase, that could be enormously counterproductive. The most obvious solution to the problem is one that many Russians fear—to open the country's doors to immigrants searching for a better life outside of their homelands. It is highly unlikely that existing birthrates among Russians will change in the foreseeable future. Therefore, the country has little choice but to encourage immigration.

If there is a term that defines Russia's future, it would be *cooperation*. Without cooperation, Russia will stagnate. Russia must become much better integrated into the global economy, which can occur through participation in the World Trade Organization. Political cooperation will stabilize internal issues and expand connections with neighboring countries and worldwide. This in turn will help further improvements in the social sphere, especially the quality of life among ordinary people. Economic prosperity and the existence of democratic institutions will minimize ethnic conflicts. Through the process of interaction, Russians will realize that cooperation, rather than isolation, generates positive results. Nothing, however, happens overnight and both patience and discipline will be required. If, as a unified outward-looking people, Russians can successfully accomplish this process of cultural change, the country can be one of the world's leaders within a matter of decades.

Facts at a Glance

Physical Geography

Location Northern Asia (the area west of the Urals is considered part of Europe), bordering the Arctic Ocean, between Europe and the North Pacific Ocean

Area Total: 6,592,894 million square miles (17,075,200 million square kilometers); land: 6,562,238 square miles (16,995,800 square kilometers); approximately the size of the North American continent; water: 30,657 square miles (79,400 square kilometers); slightly smaller than Iowa

Climate Semiarid hot, semiarid cold, humid semitropical, continental in several combinations of summer and winter conditions, polar tundra, and altitudinal climates

Terrain Glacier-created plains with low hills west of the Ural Mountains, vast lowlands and coniferous-forested mountains in Siberia, and high mountains and broad uplands along the southern border

Elevation Extremes Lowest point is the Caspian Sea, -92 feet (-28 meters); highest point is Gora (Mount) Elbrus, in the Caucasus Mountains, 18,481 feet (5,633 meters)

Land Use Arable land, 17.17%; permanent crops, 0.11%; other, 92.72% (2005)

Irrigated Land, 17,761 square miles (46,000 square kilometers) (2003)

Natural Hazards Permafrost over much of Siberia is a major impediment to development; volcanic activity in the Kuril Islands; volcanoes and earthquakes on the Kamchatka Peninsula; spring floods and summer/autumn forest fires throughout Siberia and parts of European Russia

Environmental Issues Air pollution from heavy industry, emissions of coal-fired electric plants, and transportation in major cities; industrial, municipal, and agricultural pollution of inland waterways and seacoasts; deforestation; soil erosion; soil contamination from improper application of agricultural chemicals; scattered areas of sometimes intense radioactive contamination; groundwater contamination from toxic waste; urban solid waste management; abandoned stocks of obsolete pesticides

People

Population	142,893,540 (2006 est.); males, 66,213,663 (2006 est.); females, 76,679,877 (2006 est.)
Population Density	21.65 people per square mile (8.36 per square kilometer)
Population Growth Rate	-0.37% (2006 est.)
Net Migration Rate	1.03 migrant(s)/1,000 population (2006 est.)
Fertility Rate	1.28 children born/woman (2006 est.)
Life Expectancy at Birth	Total population: 67.08 years; male, 60.45 years; female, 74.10 years (2006 est.)
Median Age	38.4 years; male, 35.2 years; female, 41.3 years (2006 est.)
Ethnic Groups	Russians, 79.8%; Tatars, 3.8%; Ukrainians, 2.0%; Bashkirs, 1.2%; Chuvash, 1.1%; others, 12.1%
Religions	Russian Orthodox, 15–20%; Muslim, 10–15%; other Christian, 2%
Languages	Russian, Tatar, and Ukrainian (and many others, some of which have fewer than 5,000 speakers).
Literacy	(age 15 and over can read and write) Total population: Estimated to be 99.6% (male, 99.7%; female, 99.5%) (2003 est.)

Economy

Currency	Russian ruble (RUR)
GDP Purchasing Power Parity (PPP)	$1.589 trillion (2005 est.)
GDP Per Capita (PPP)	$11,100 (2005 est.)
Labor Force	74.22 million (2005 est.)
Unemployment	7.6%, plus considerable underemployment (2005 est.)
Labor Force by Occupation	Services, 68.3%; industry, 21.4%; agriculture, 10.3%
Agricultural Products	Grain, sugar beets, sunflower seed, vegetables, fruits; beef, milk
Industries	Complete range of mining and extractive industries producing coal, oil, gas, chemicals, and metals; all forms of machine building from rolling mills to high-performance aircraft and space vehicles; defense industries including radar, missile production, and advanced electronic components, shipbuilding; road and rail transportation equipment; communications equipment; agricultural machinery, tractors, and construction equipment; electric power generating and transmitting

	equipment; medical and scientific instruments; consumer durables, textiles, foodstuffs, and handicrafts
Exports	$245 billion (2005 est.)
Imports	$125 billion (2005 est.)
Leading Trade Partners	Exports: Netherlands, 10.3%; Germany, 8.3%; Italy, 7.9%; China, 5.5%; Ukraine, 5.2%; Turkey, 4.5%; Switzerland, 4.4% (2005). Imports: Germany, 13.6%; Ukraine, 8%; China, 7.4%; Japan, 6%; Belarus, 4.7%; U.S., 4.7%; Italy, 4.6%; South Korea, 4.1% (2005)
Export Commodities	Petroleum and petroleum products, natural gas, wood and wood products, metals, chemicals, and a wide variety of civilian and military manufactures
Import Commodities	Machinery and equipment, consumer goods, medicines, meat, sugar, semifinished metal products
Transportation	Roadways: 541,239 miles (871,000 kilometers), of which 458,593 miles (738,000 kilometers) are paved (2004); Airports: 1,623, including 616 with paved runways (2006); Waterways: 63,383 miles (102,000 kilometers)

Government

Country Name	Conventional long form: Russian Federation; Conventional short form: Russia; Local long form: Rossiyskaya Federatsiya; Local short form: Rossiya; Former: Russian Empire, Russian Soviet Federative Socialist Republic
Capital City	Moscow
Type of Government	Federation
Head of Government	Premier Mikhail Yefimovich Fradkov (since March 5, 2004); chief of state is President Vladimir Vladimirovich Putin (since May 7, 2000)
Independence	August 24, 1991 (from the Soviet Union)
Administrative Divisions	48 oblasts; 21 republics; 9 autonomous okrugs; 7 krays; 2 federal cities; and 1 autonomous oblast

Communications

TV stations	7,306 (1999)
Phones	(Line) 40,100,000; (cell) 120,000,000 (2005)
Internet Users	23,700,000 (2005)

* Source: CIA-The World Factbook (2006)

122

Moscow

1147	First written record of Moscow.
1359–1389	Kremlin of Moscow begun; Moscow defeats the Tatars in 1378.
1462–1505	Ivan III (the Great) rules.
1463–1489	Many cities incorporated into Moscow.
1485–1516	Building of new Kremlin.
1502	Destruction of Golden Horde by Crimean Tatars.
1533–1584	Ivan IV (the Terrible) reigns–first Russian sovereign to be crowned tsar (in 1547, in the Kremlin's Uspensky Cathedral).
1581	Beginning of the conquest of Siberia.
1598–1610	Time of Troubles.

The Romanovs

1613–1645	Reign of Michael (elected by the Zemsky Sobor).
1645–1676	Reign of Alexis.
1653	Last Zemsky Sobor summoned to vote on the incorporation of Ukraine.
1682–1725	Reign of Peter the Great; in the first outward-looking reign in Russian history, Peter opens a window on Western ideas; techniques flood into Russia.
1701–1703	Founding of St. Petersburg.
1721	Peter adopts the title of emperor.
1762–1796	Reign of Catherine II (the Great), wife of Peter III.
1772	First partition of Poland occurs.
1773–1774	Pugachev's revolt.
1781–1786	Ukraine absorbed completely into Russian Empire; annexation of the Crimea.
1783	Russian protectorship over eastern Georgia.
1784	Settlement in Alaska; second (1793) and third (1795) partitions of Poland.
1796–1801	Reign of Paul I; enacts a new law on succession based on male primogeniture.

1801–1825	Reign of Alexander I.
1812	Napoleon and Battle of Borodino, burning of Moscow, pursuit of retreating Napoleon into France.
1825	Revolt, sometimes called the first Russian Revolution, in December.
1825–1855	Nicholas I, a reactionary tsar, rules.
1826	Organization of political police force; first Russian railway opened between St. Petersburg and Tsarkoye Selo.
1855–1881	Reign of Alexander II, "The Tsar Liberator," a reforming tsar.
1861	Emancipation of serfs.
1867	Sale of Alaska to the United States; first Russian translation of Karl Marx's *Das Kapital*.
1881	Alexander II accepts proposal for a committee for reform and is assassinated the same day.
1881–1894	Reign of Alexander III, conservative and nationalist like his grandfather Nicholas I.
1891	Construction of the Trans-Siberian Railroad begins.
1894–1917	Nicholas II, the last Russian tsar, marries Queen Victoria's granddaughter Princess Alix of Hessen-Darmstadt.
1900	Social Democratic Labor Party splits into two factions—Bolsheviks (majoritarians), led by Lenin, and Mensheviks (minoritarians), led by Martov.
1904	Japan attacks Russia at Port Arthur without declaring war.
1905	Revolution of 1905; internal economic grievances, government failure to cope with needs of a growing industrial society, and the defeat of Russia by the Japanese lead to mass violence by the Russian people and concessions from the tsar.
1906	Opening of first Duma, or Parliament, containing both Bolsheviks and Mensheviks.
1911	Prime Minister Pyotr Stolypin assassinated.

1914–1918	War and Revolution.
1914	Outbreak of World War I, which Lenin sees as a chance for revolution.
1917	February Revolution; abdication of Nicholas II; October Revolution (November 6–7); Lenin, leading Bolshevik faction, overthrows the provisional government in Petrograd in a bloodless coup; issues decree nationalizing all private, ecclesiastical, and tsarist land without compensation; the tsar and his family are murdered at Ekaterinburg; end of Russian participation in World War I.
1918–1924	Civil War and Communism.
1918–1920	Bolsheviks introduce press censorship, nationalize heavy industry, outlaw strikes, nationalize banks, build up police force (the Cheka) and Red Army, and organize requisition of grain for army and urban population; engage in civil war with White Army.
1921	Famine; Tenth Party Congress introduces New Economic Policy, giving peasants freedom in cultivating their land and marketing produce, while state retains control of industry, foreign trade, banking, and transport; Union of Soviet Socialist Republics (Soviet Union) established.
1924	Lenin dies; Petrograd renamed "Leningrad" in his honor.
The Stalin Years	
1924–1938	Stalin asserts his supremacy.
1928–1929	First Five-Year Plan and start of collectivization.
1930	Industrialization takes precedence over collectivization; disorganization of agriculture leads to famine.
1939–1945	World War II.
1939	Soviet–Nazi Nonaggression Pact.
1941	Soviet Union enters "Great Patriotic War" when Germany invades.
1945	Russians enter Hungary, Poland, and Austria; **May 2**: capture of Berlin.
1945–1953	Occupation of Eastern Europe enables Communist governments to come to power in Poland, Hungary, Bulgaria, Czechoslovakia, and Yugoslavia.

| 1946 | Famine in Ukraine. |
| **March 1953** | Stalin dies; **June:** uprising in East Berlin smashed by Soviet tanks. |

The Khrushchev Years

1953–1964	Nikita Khrushchev becomes first secretary of Soviet Communist Party.
1956	**February:** Twentieth Party Congress hears Khrushchev's "secret speech" denouncing Stalin.
1958	**March:** Khrushchev takes over premiership from Bulganin.
1961	**April:** Cosmonaut Yuri Gagarin becomes first man in space aboard Vostok 1.
1964	Khrushchev's resignation demanded by his colleagues.

Brezhnev and After

1964–1982	Leonid Brezhnev succeeds Khrushchev as party secretary.
1979	Afghanistan invaded by Soviet Union.
1982	Brezhnev dies.
1982–1991	Sixty-eight-year-old Yuri Andropov succeeds Brezhnev, but dies in **February 1984**; Konstantin Chernenko, a 72-year-old protégé of Brezhnev, becomes party secretary amid rumors of power struggles; **March 1985**: Chernenko dies; 54-year-old Mikhail Gorbachev is elected general secretary by Central Committee; Gorbachev campaigns energetically to move Soviet economy forward and appears to favor new style of leadership that includes informal contact with people at home and abroad.

Russian Federation

| 1991 | Boris Yeltsin becomes the first democratically elected Russian president; Gorbachev resigns as head of the Communist Party; Yeltsin disbands the Communist Party; the Soviet Union is dissolved and the Commonwealth of Independent States (CIS) created; the Soviet Union ceases to exist on December 25. |

1994 Russian troops invade Chechnya; social services in great disarray.

1998 Russian financial crisis; crime soars.

2000 Vladimir Putin elected president of the Russian Federation; polls of Russian citizens support Putin and his planned reforms.

2001 Putin pledges support of U.S. actions to combat terrorism and expresses condolences for those who were injured or died in the terrorist acts on September 11.

2002 President Putin and U.S. president George W. Bush sign landmark nuclear arms reduction treaty called the Moscow Treaty.

2004 Putin reelected as Russian Federation president.

2005 Government records $56 billion in budget surplus.

2006 Russia's gold and foreign currency reserves top $250 billion.

Glossary

Your study of Russia will be more interesting if you take time to use this glossary. The letters that appear inside brackets following each word show you how the word should sound when it is correctly pronounced. The capital letters used to indicate the pronunciation show you which syllable of the word is to receive the chief stress, as: Angara (un ga RA).

black earth soils: Highly fertile soil, rich in organic matter, commonly found beneath midlatitude grasslands.

Bolshevik (BOHL shuh vihk) Party: A group of people in Imperial Russia who believed that Communist governments should be established throughout the world by revolution. The Bolsheviks (also called Communists) gained control of the Russian government in 1917.

Brezhnev (brezh NYUHF), Leonid I., 1906–1982: Soviet leader who succeeded Khrushchev as head of the Communist Party in October 1964.

capitalism: A system in which individual people or private corporations own land, factories, and other property used to make a living.

Catherine II, 1729–1796, called Catherine the Great: A German princess who married the heir to the Russian throne when she was 16. She forced him from the throne in 1762 and became ruler.

Commonwealth of Independent States (CIS): Organization formed following the breakup of the Soviet Union, comprising the Russian Federation and 11 other former Soviet republics. Estonia, Latvia, and Lithuania did not join.

Communism: A term used to describe a way of living in which all land and other property is owned by the community. Also refers to the teachings and actions of the Soviet Communist Party and of the Communist parties in other countries.

Communist Revolution: Also known as the Bolshevik Revolution or Russian Revolution. The revolution of November 1917 that brought the Communists to power in Russia.

cooperative: In the Soviet Union, an enterprise, such as a collective farm or industrial producers' cooperative, in which the equipment and buildings are owned in common by the people who work there.

Cyrillic (sih RIHL ihk) alphabet: The alphabet used in writing Russian.

glasnost (GLAS nohst): Gorbachev's policy in the late 1980s, designed to create greater information openness in the Soviet Union.

Gorbachev (gor bih CHOF), Mikhail, 1931– : Led the Soviet Union during its final years, from 1985 to 1991. Elevated younger party members to leadership. Introduced openness (glasnost) and restructuring (perestroika) in an attempt to compete with the West.

Ivan IV, 1530–1584, called Ivan the Terrible: The first Russian ruler to be crowned tsar.

Khrushchev (KROOSH chef), Nikita Sergeevich, 1894–1971: From 1958 to 1964, head of both the Communist Party and the government of the Soviet Union. Other Communist leaders removed Khrushchev from power in October 1964.

Kremlin (KREM lihn): Walled fortress in the heart of Moscow. It is the seat of the Russian government.

Lenin (LEN ihn), Vladimir Ilyich, 1870–1924: Real name was Vladimir Ilyich Ulyanov. Spent most of his life working to overthrow the imperial Russian government. Led the Communist Revolution of November 1917, and became the leader of the new government. Is called the founder of the Soviet Union.

Marx, Karl, 1818–1883: A German thinker who believed that the working-class people throughout the world would someday unite to overthrow their old governments and replace them with Communism. (See Communism.) He is sometimes called the father of modern Communism. Was exiled from Germany because of his revolutionary activities and spent his last years in England.

Nicholas II, 1868–1918: The last tsar to rule Russia. Was forced to leave his throne by the revolution of March 1917.

perestroika (pehr ah STROY ka): Gorbachev's policy in the late 1980s, designed to restructure the political and economic systems of the Soviet Union.

Peter I, 1672–1725, called Peter the Great: A powerful Russian tsar who often used brutal methods to bring modern ways to his country. He founded the city of St. Petersburg.

Politburo: The highest governing body of the Soviet Communist Party. The head of the Politburo was the general secretary (later changed to first secretary), who was the leader of the Soviet Communist Party.

presidium: In the Soviet Union, a committee that directed the work of the government.

privatization: Sale of state-owned enterprises to private owners.

Putin (POO tihn), Vladimir, 1952– : From 2000 to the present, president of the Russian Federation. Reasserted central government authority over various republics and regions. Pledged support of U.S. actions to combat terrorism.

Russian Orthodox Church: Refers to one of three main branches of Christianity. This branch consists of a loosely connected group of independent churches located mainly in western Asia and eastern Europe. This group of churches (also called the Eastern Orthodox Church) separated from the Roman Catholic Church in 1054.

St. Petersburg: Second-largest city in Russia. Founded by Peter the Great. Was called St. Petersburg until 1914, when its name was changed to Petrograd. After Lenin's death, it was named Leningrad. Name returned to St. Petersburg following the breakup of the Soviet Union.

serf: A person who was similar to a slave, in that he or she was not allowed to leave the land on which he or she worked.

Siberia (si BEER ee uh): The northern part of Asia that stretches from the Ural Mountains to the Pacific Ocean.

Slavs (SLAHVZ): A large group of people who speak similar languages. They are descendants of the early Slavs who lived near the western borders of Russia when Jesus Christ was born. Russians, Poles, and Bulgarians all belong to the Slavic group of people.

Soviet Union: Official name is Union of Soviet Socialist Republics (USSR). A Communist country spanning northeastern Europe to northeastern Asia that emerged following the 1917 Revolution against imperial Russia. Split into 15 independent republics in 1991.

Stalin (STAH lihn), Joseph, 1879–1953: Real name was Iosif Vissarionovich Dzhugashvili. Was the son of a shoemaker in Imperial Russian Georgia. Before the Communist Revolution, he was exiled many times for working against the government. After Lenin's death, he overcame other rivals to become the dictator of the Soviet Union.

tsar (ZAHR): The title used by the rulers of Russia from the sixteenth century until the revolution of March 1917.

Vikings (VI kings): Daring Scandinavian warriors who raided the coasts of Europe from about A.D. 800 to 1050.

Yeltsin (YELT sihn), Boris, 1931– : From 1991 to 1999, president of the Russian Federation. First democratically elected Russian president. Strengthened the powers of the president.

Aeroflot-International Airlines. AEROFLOT, Russian International Airlines. Available online at *http://www.aeroflot.org/*

Afanasev, Aleksandr. *Russian Fairy Tales.* New York: Pantheon Books, 1976.

Barbour, William, and Carol Wekesser, eds. *The Breakup of the Soviet Union: Opposing Viewpoints.* San Diego, Calif.: Greenhaven Press, 1994.

Central Intelligence Agency. The World Factbook 2006. Available online at *http://www.cia.gov/cia/publications/factbook/index.html*

Cominfo. Virtual Tour of Moscow Kremlin. Available online at *http://www.moscowkremlin.ru/NS/english/*

Goskomstat. State Committee of the Russian Federation on Statistics. Available online at *http://www.gks.ru/eng/*

Holmes, Burton, and Fred L. Israel et al., eds. *Moscow (World 100 Years Ago).* Philadelphia: Chelsea House Publishers, 1998.

Johnson Space Center. The Gateway to Astronaut Photography of Earth. Available online at *http://eol.jsc.nasa.gov/sseop*

Moscow Times.com. Available online at *http://www.moscowtimes.ru*

Otfinoski, Steven. *Boris Yeltsin and the Rebirth of Russia.* Brookfield, Conn.: Millbrook Press, 1995.

Rosaviakosmos. Russian Aviation and Space Agency. Available online at *http://www.rosaviakosmos.ru/english/eindex.htm*

Russian Cities on the Web. Available online at *http://www.city.ru/*

St. Petersburg Times, General News from St. Petersburg and Russia. Available online at *http://www.sptimes.ru/*

Sigachyov, Sergey. *The Trans-Siberian Railway Web Encyclopedia.* Available online at http://www.transsib.ru/Eng/

State Hermitage Museum, St. Petersburg, Russia. Available online at *http://www.hermitagemuseum.org/html_En/index.html*

Streissguth, Thomas. *Soviet Leaders from Lenin to Gorbachev.* Minneapolis, Minn.: Oliver Press, 1992.

Toht, Patricia, and Bob Moulder. *Daily Life in Ancient and Modern Moscow.* Minneapolis, Minn.: Runestone Press, 2000.

Vail, John J. *Peace, Land, Bread: A History of the Russian Revolution.* New York: Facts on File, 1996.

Verne, Jules. *Michael Strogoff: A Courier of the Czar.* New York: Atheneum, 1997.

Further Reading

Kort, Michael. *Russia, Third Edition.* New York: Infobase Publishing, 2004.

McCray, Thomas. *Russia and the Former Soviet Republics.* New York: Infobase Publishing, 2006.

Service, Robert. *A History of Modern Russia: From Nicholas II to Vladimir Putin.* Cambridge, Mass.: Harvard University Press, 2005.

Shaw, Dennis. *Russia in the Modern World.* Oxford, UK: Blackwell Publishing, 2005.

Shields, Charles J. *Vladimir Putin.* New York: Infobase Publishing, 2007.

Web sites

CIA—The World Factbook
https://www.cia.gov/cia/publications/factbook/geos/rs.html

U.S. Department of State—Russia
http://www.state.gov/r/pa/ei/bgn/3183.htm

Index

Index

Index

Picture Credits

WILLIAM A. DANDO is emeritus professor of geography, geology, and anthropology at Indiana State University. He has devoted his career to the study of food and famine, with particular reference to the former Soviet Union. Professor Dando has traveled to the former USSR on many occasions. He has authored a number of books, chapters, and professional articles covering a variety of geographic topics.

ZORAN PAVLOVIĆ is a cultural geographer currently working at Oklahoma State University in Stillwater. *Russia* is the tenth book Pavlović authored, coauthored, or contributed to for the Chelsea House geography series MODERN WORLD NATIONS. He also authored *Europe* for the MODERN WORLD CULTURES series. In geography, his interests are culture theory, evolution of geographic thought, and geography of viticulture. He was born and raised in southeastern Europe.

CHARLES F. GRITZNER is distinguished professor of geography at South Dakota State University in Brookings. He is now in his fifth decade of college teaching, research, and writing. In addition to teaching, he enjoys writing, working with teachers, and sharing his love of geography with readers. As the series editor for Chelsea House's MODERN WORLD NATIONS (and other) series, he has had a wonderful opportunity to combine these interests. Dr. Gritzner has served as both president and executive director of the National Council for Geographic Education. He also has received many national honors, including the George J. Miller Award for Distinguished Service to Geographic Education from the NCGE and both the Distinguished Teaching Achievement Award and the Gilbert Grosvenor Honors in Geographic Education from the Association of American Geographers.